A Faith for Generations

A Family Prayer Guide in the Anglican Tradition

Edited and Updated
in Language
with Additions by

Deacon Andrew E. Brashier

Archdeacon Books
A Publishing Imprint of Woody Norman LLC
Hoover, Alabama 35244

Commentary Copyright © 2019
by Andrew England Brashier

All rights reserved, including the right to reproduce this book
or portions thereof in any form whatsoever without the expressed consent of the
publisher and the author.
For information
contact via email woody.norman@gmail.com.

The WOODY NORMAN LLC Speakers Bureau can book any
of its published authors to your live event. For information,
contact via email woody.norman@gmail.com.

Names: Andrew England Brashier, editor
Title: A Faith for Generations/A Family Prayer Guide in the Anglican
Tradition/Andrew England Brashier.
Description: Paperback edition.
Hoover, Alabama: Archdeacon Books, 2019.

ISBN 978-1949422-81-8

BISAC: Religion/Bible/New Testament

Contents

Contents i
Foreword v
Introduction ix

PART ONE

ESSAYS ON FAMILY PRAYER AND ANGLICANISM 1
  Family Prayer: An Uncommon Habit 2
  Starting a Family Oratory 6
  Teach Your Children Well 8
  The Need for Common Prayer and Family Oratories 13
  Every Home a Chapel Common Prayer in Practice 18
  Catechesis through Singing 23
  Reformation, Authority, Anglicanism, and the Home Oratory 26
  The Home as a Monastery 33

PART TWO

FAMILY DEVOTIONS 36
FAMILY OFFICE 36
  MORNING PRAYER 36
    Acknowledgment of God's Mercy and Preservation through the Night 37
    Dedication of Soul and Body to God's Service 37
    For Grace to guide and keep us the following Day, and for God's Blessing 38
    For God's blessing upon the business of the day 39
    Confession of Sins, with a Prayer for Contrition and Pardon 41
    Prayer for Grace to reform and grow better 42
    The Intercession 43
    The Thanksgiving 44

    Prayer for God's Protection through the Night following............................ 44
A SHORTER FORM OF THE FAMILY DAILY OFFICES....... 46
    MORNING... 46
A SHORTER FORM OF THE FAMILY DAILY OFFICES....... 47
    EVENING.. 47
AN ORDER FOR PRIVATE INDIVIDUAL 48
    MORNING PRAYER... 48
AN ORDER FOR PRIVATE INDIVIDUAL 50
    EVENING PRAYER.. 50
ADDITIONAL PRAYERS 52
    For the Spirit of Prayer 52
    In the Morning 52
    At Night 53
    Sunday Morning 53
    For Quiet Confidence 53
    For Guidance 54
    For Trustfulness 54
    For Joy in God's Creation 55
    For the Children 55
    For the Absent 55
    For Those We Love 56
    For the Recovery of a Sick Person 56
    For One about to undergo an Operation 56
    For a Birthday 56
    For an Anniversary of One Departed 57
    For Those in Mental Darkness 57
    For a Blessing on the Families of the Land 57
    For all Poor, Homeless, and the Neglected 58

For Faithfulness in the Use of this World's Goods 58
A General Intercession 59
Grace before Meat 59

PART THREE

EDITOR'S NOTE: 60
GODLY PRAYERS 61
A general confession of sins, to be said every morning 61
Prayers to be said in the Morning 63
A prayer against temptation 64
A prayer for the obtaining of wisdom 65
A prayer against worldly cares 66
A prayer necessary for all persons 66
A prayer necessary to be said at all times 68
Miscellaneous Daily Prayers 70
A prayer for trust in God 72
A prayer for the concord of Christ's church 73
A prayer against the enemies of Christ's truth 74
A prayer for patience in trouble 74
A prayer to be said at night going to bed 75
A prayer to be said at the hour of death 75
Another prayer for the Morning 77
A prayer for the Evening 77
The prayer of Manasseh King of the Jews 79
A Prayer containing the duty of every true Christian 81

PART FOUR

THE CLASSIC BOOK OF COMMON PRAYER CATECHISM – A MODERNIZED TEXT 83

A Catechism 85
Acknowledgements 93

Foreword

The Anglican Church in North America (ACNA) recently published its 2019 *Book of Common Prayer* (BCP). By all accounts, it is an incredible work – eliminating many of the theological concerns of the 1979 Prayer Book and other similar attempts. In the course of researching historic prayer books and supplementary prayer books to ensure the catholicity of historic Christian orthodoxy and orthopraxy, there were many elements of older writings that were "rediscovered" that belong in the library of any Christian who is devoted to prayer. Among these works is, of course, the 1662 *Book of Common Prayer*.

The Reverend Andrew Brashier is a respected attorney and the Chancellor for the Jurisdiction of the Armed Forces and Chaplaincy. He also serves on several prominent boards and committees with the ACNA and several ministries. It is no surprise that Deacon Andrew followed very closely the seminal work of the ACNA's Liturgy Task Force commissioned to the work of the new Prayer Book. It is important to remember that the BCP is not just a worship service book, but rather a book for our everyday lives. As part of Deacon Andrew's personal "rediscovery" was the emphasis placed on family prayer in earlier works. With so many things – television, internet, entertainment, activities, etc. – to distract us from a vibrant prayer life at home, Deacon Andrew took this rediscovery as a challenge. Families are called to emulate the prayer practices experienced in the church. The head of the household is provided an immense task and vocation: disciple the family in their relationship with our great high priest, Jesus Christ. The life of prayer is a life of formation and learning to live our Lord's commands that cannot be lost to the Church but must also be a practice and discipline in the home. To love the Lord our God with all our heart, soul, mind, and strength and to love our neighbors truly as ourselves cannot be fully understood in a once or twice a week gathering. It must be a daily family routine.

So out of this rediscovery comes this work of love to which Deacon Andrew has been committed over the last several years. He has revisited, in modern language, the historical prayers of the classic 1662 *Book of Common Prayer*'s catechism for the consumption of families and those interested in the prayer life of the Anglican church shortly after its Reformation. This may perhaps be the first "supplemental" reading to the new Prayer Book. This work by Deacon Andrew is commendable for providing a historical resource for those who would like to take a deeper look at the prayers from the Anglican Church that served families and individuals for decades, not to mention the classic catechism that is a part of the Anglican formularies.

May the reader of this work be inspired to pick up their *Book of Common Prayer* and pray daily. May you be blessed and inspired by these Anglican prayers of old in addition to Deacon Andrew's practical suggestions for creating a regular family practice and discipline of family prayer and devotion.

On this 11th day of November, In the Year of our Lord, 2019, The Feast of St. Martin of Tours.

In Nomine Iesus,

The Right Reverend Derek LS Jones
First Bishop of the Armed Forces and Chaplaincy
The Jurisdiction of the Armed Forces and Chaplaincy
of the Anglican Church in North America

Introduction

This book begins with a selection of essays providing practical advice for families beginning the habit of daily prayer. This advice is merely based upon my own personal experience and derives from material originally published on my blog, *We See Through a Mirror Darkly* (www.thruamirrordarkly.wordpress.com).[1] It is my intent that this section explain how to create a regular family prayer life and encourage laity on how to develop a habit of common prayer. I credit Bishop Edmund Gibson for his original work on family and individual devotions for spurring me to write those essays and, in turn, this book. The committee that drafted the 1928 *Book of Common Prayer* should be commended for adopting many of the prayers he authored into the Family Prayers section of that prayer book.

It is interesting that Bishop Edmund Gibson took the step to create a book of individual prayers dedicated for use throughout his diocese considering Anglicans are typically known for the corporate prayers enshrined in the *Book of Common Prayer*. Bishop Gibson's family prayer devotional was originally addressed towards servants who were not always allowed inside the family's worship and were too far away or consumed with their duties to attend distance church services in the closest country parish. It is also evident that Bishop Gibson developed these extensive prayers to serve the

---

[1] The blog still exists but new content has been moved to *The North American Anglican* (www.northamanglican.com).

American frontier, since all Anglican churches in the colonies were under his purview as Bishop of London. In regard to his concern as to American colonists, Bishop Gibson shared a common interest with Anglican priests John and Charles Wesley. Although the Wesley brothers were active and contemporaneous with Bishop Gibson, he did not join the new "Methodists" although he shared some of their concerns and goals.

The language Bishop Gibson utilizes is beautiful in both its wording and theological depth. I personally rather not alter the wording, but since the ACNA[2] 2019 *Book of Common Prayer* is in contemporary language, I believe a gentle "modernizing" (I hate that word) of Bishop Gibson's devotions is worthwhile and necessary given the paucity of the Family Prayer section in the proposed ACNA 2019 *Book of Common Prayer*.

Although I submitted a modernized version of part of Bishop Gibson's work (the same as found in the 1928 *Book of Common Prayer*) to the ACNA Liturgy Task Force, the ACNA ultimately opted to lightly revise the Family Prayer section of the Episcopal Church's 1979 *Book of Common Prayer*. Therefore, I was compelled to submit this more extensive work for publication, so it may assist families and individuals everywhere who need guidance in devoting themselves to regular prayer.

---

[2] Anglican Church in North America

During my work on this project, I discovered a selection of prayers commonly appended to the 1559 *Book of Common Prayer* during Queen Elizabeth I's reign, that are entitled "Godly Prayers." These prayers have also been republished in this work and are also slightly updated for contemporary audiences. Also included in this work is a "modernized" language version of the classic catechism from the 1662 *Book of Common Prayer*. This is included so parents can teach their children the fundamentals necessary for confirmation. The ACNA Catechism is an expansive work that is needed in these post-Christian times which we find ourselves in. However, it is also a voluminous work that is more extensive than what a young child is required to learn for confirmation.

Unfortunately, family prayer and catechesis are ignored by the average American Christian. This should not be a surprise considering the average church has abandoned a formal prayer book and formal catechesis. Therefore, the past two generations of Christians are unfamiliar with their own faith, much less using the formal prayers of the tradition to guide their prayer life. The following condensed Daily Office and Prayers for Families is meant to encourage laity to take up their responsibilities to the Lord in raising disciples within the home. It is imperative that ACNA, and every orthodox Anglican and Christian jurisdiction, take up the banner of Christian catechesis and family prayer. Laity are called to be outposts of heaven through regular prayer and teaching the Holy Scriptures to their own households. Should families develop each of their homes into private chapels of prayer then they will bolster and strengthen the life of the local parish. In time active families will reach out to new Christians or non-believers who are struggling with a life of prayer and need proper catechesis into the faith.

Finally, a word to fathers and mothers. Parents, our vocations are not merely limited to our careers but extend to fatherhood and motherhood. Through the prayers presented herein, parents are able to bless, praise, and petition our Lord in prayer while providing an example to our children. By teaching our children (and ourselves) how to pray, we will be teaching our children the faith the Church professes and how to discern the depths of doctrine from the perils of error. May the Lord use this work to bless your family and your own growth into the New Man as we shed off the old Adam.

In Christ,

Deacon Andrew E. Brashier
Chancellor, Jurisdiction of the Armed Forces
    and Chaplaincy
Vicar, Anglican Church of the Good Shepherd,
    Pelham, Alabama
Sinner, and by God's grace, redeemed as His Servant.

Part One

ESSAYS ON FAMILY PRAYER AND ANGLICANISM

The following are articles originally published on my personal blog and that have been edited and updated to provide guidance and encourage the reader to begin having regular family devotions. I suggest networking with other families to form a small group dedicated to the common rule and doctrine of classical Anglicanism as laid out in the *Book of Common Prayer*. Additionally, I hope for the many new Anglicans who are coming into ACNA, that this serves as a resource as to learning more about Anglican theology and practice. May it assist in guiding you to take on the discipline of the prayer book and be formed into a disciple of Jesus Christ in the Anglican way.

Please note these short essays were drafted over the period of several years and you will see how my own family's devotions have slight changes – typically to better fit the age of my own children and how they learn best.

Family Prayer: An Uncommon Habit

Habits are common, but a good habit requires discipline. One does not fall into a good habit but falling into a bad habit is as easy as rolling downhill. Discipline is what makes good habits uncommon. Perhaps the most uncommon habit, yet the most important, is prayer.

Prayer is sadly neglected all too often in the life of the average Christian, I myself being no exception. Therefore, I rejoice at the great resource that is the *Book of Common Prayer*. Its prayers are directed to the Triune God, in gentle rebuke to my inwardly focused prayers which can ramble with only invoking the Father. As a tool, the *Book of Common Prayer* (BCP) can develop the uncommon habit of prayer. The regular use of the daily offices of morning and evening prayer will quickly lead one to learn a multitude of Psalms, hymns, Scripture, and collects that truly "collect" one's mind towards God and neighbor. Even irregular use of the offices in the *Book of Common Prayer* will quickly assist in learning the Apostles' Creed and the Lord's Prayer.

Developing the uncommon habit of common prayer is not limited to the individual. Those called to raise families have a great responsibility as the basic unit of the church. As a Christian who is learning daily what it means to be a father, I have appreciated the guidance of the *Book of Common Prayer* in disciplining my regular prayers. Prayer is an uncommon habit and family prayer even more so. It is an awkward (and even uncomfortable) discipline to develop within a family, but we are called to raise our families in the faith and have promised to do so before the church in the baptism service:

> *Minister.* Having now, in the name of this Child, made these promises, will ye also on your part take heed that he learn the Creed, the Lord's Prayer, and the Ten Commandments, and all other things which a Christian ought to know and believe, to his soul's health?
>
> *Answer.* I will, by God's help.
>
> *Minister.* Will ye take heed that this Child, so soon as sufficiently instructed, be brought to the Bishop to be confirmed by him?
>
> *Answer.* I will, God being my helper.
> (1928 *Book of Common Prayer* Baptism service).[3]

---

[3] The ACNA 2019 *Book of Common Prayer* requires the same in addition to knowing the longer ACNA Catechism, which has not been published in its final form as of publication of this book. It states:

"Dearly beloved, it is essential that those who wish to be Confirmed or Received in this Church publicly confess Jesus Christ as their Lord and Savior; become his disciples; know and affirm the Nicene Creed, the Lord's Prayer, and the Ten Commandments; and have received instruction in the Holy Scriptures of the Old and New Testaments and the Catechism of the Church."

See ACNA 2019 *Book of Common Prayer*, p. 176.

Therefore, it is imperative that we establish family prayer in our homes. The emphasis should not merely be to get through an office, but to bring the family together in prayer. Family prayer is uniquely flexible within the 1928 and ACNA *Book of Common Prayer*, so one can use as few or as many prayers as best for your family.

I recommend always reciting the Creed, praying the Lord's Prayer, and singing the Doxology as three standards in every family's devotional routine. Simply reciting these three for children at a young age will assist memorizing the basics of the faith—foundations that will always remain with them. Additionally, covering the Creed, the Lord's Prayer, and the Doxology will assist children in preparation for confirmation. When my daughter was three years old, she was able to sing the Doxology and recite portions of the Lord's Prayer due to regular evening devotions. Throughout the year my wife and I continued teaching her about the meaning of the Apostles' Creed, the Lord's Prayer, and the Doxology. Slowly, we will add additional prayers, collects, portions of the catechism, and readings so that our use of the *Book of Common Prayer* will grow as our family grows. By the time she turned four, my daughter learned the Lord's Prayer and almost had the Apostles' Creed memorized by heart.

The *Book of Common Prayer*, along with the classic prayers and modernized 1662 prayer book catechism republished in this book, are tools Christian families can use to develop a rule of prayer. The prayer book is a priceless treasure that organizes Scripture into prayer and is rooted in the ancient way of the church. The practice of common prayer will develop an uncommon habit, namely communion with the Triune God. Over time, dedication to nurturing habitual prayer will become second nature and you will find yourself formed by the prayers and the prayers becoming a part of yourself and your family.

Note: I also recommend the Reformed Episcopal Church (REC) 2003 edition of the *Book of Common Prayer* as it provides an abbreviated version of the daily offices in its Family Prayer section that is based upon the 1928 American prayer book. The REC even offers a Modern Language edition of their prayer book although it sadly is no longer published physically but remains available online.[4]

---

[4] 2003 Reformed Episcopal Church *Modern Language Book of Common Prayer* can be found, as of the date of publication of this book, at: http://www.recus.org/documents/ModernLanguageBCP.pdf.

Starting a Family Oratory

I am convinced that the hardest thing about any spiritual discipline is beginning. Whether it is prayer, fasting, reading Scripture, etc. it is taking the first step in developing the habit that remains the most difficult.

Lent is a time for taking on a new discipline and starting a family oratory is an activity in which the entire family can participate. But where to start, and how? The 1928 *Book of Common Prayer's* Family Prayer section provides (and this book republishes in modern language) "A Shorter Form" version of morning and evening prayer that consist of three short prayers.

After regular use of the "Shorter Form," the family can advance to the full Family Prayer version of morning and evening prayer (which are longer and found just prior to the "Shorter Form."). Finally, as the family's children grow older, the full versions of morning and evening prayer can be used along with incorporating the church catechism (published in this book in a slightly updated language) and Thirty-Nine Articles of Religion. Essentially, the beauty of a family oratory is gradually catechizing the family.

A renewed Anglicanism will require a new generation who understand their faith and are disciplined in the habit of common prayer. The path to such a renewal begins within the home when fathers and mothers turn their house into an altar of prayer. Getting started requires a time commitment that is minimal but should be regular in order to become routine. For families with young children, I recommend either starting after dinner or just prior to bedtime and only doing the abbreviated family prayer office found in this book until you have it down pat. Then you can incorporate the office of morning prayer and move to the larger family office for morning and evening prayer and eventually to the full prayer book offices. Starting this discipline will make praying the daily offices a natural and expected part of life for your children so they will even ask to pray if you skip or forget to do an office (believe me, they will remind you if you slip up!).

The key to any new habit is discipline. Take up the habit of praying a short office and soon it will become instilled within your family and yourself as a natural extension to starting or ending your day. The goal is to ultimately do both morning and evening prayer so that as a family, we awake to praising God and go to sleep praising Him.

Teach Your Children Well

"As the head of the family should teach them in a simple way to his household."

– Luther's Small Catechism

"And all Fathers, Mothers, Masters, and Mistresses, shall cause their Children, Servants, and Apprentices, who have not learned their Catechism, to come to the Church at the time appointed, and obediently to hear and to be ordered by the Minister, until such time as they have learned all that is here appointed for them to learn."

– U.S. *Book of Common Prayer*, Catechism, 1928

The duty of the head of the household is to teach the family the catechism of the church. The catechism is not important in and of itself but draws its strength and importance as a tool insofar as it reflects the teaching of Scripture. Fortunately, both Dr. Martin Luther's Small Catechism and the catechism in the classical *Book of Common Prayer* are firmly rooted in Scripture.

Both Luther's Small Catechism and the classic prayer book catechism focus on the ancient requirement that catechumens learn the Ten Commandments, the Apostles' Creed, and the Lord's Prayer. The Ten Commandments are taught first to announce the law by which we have all fallen short. It shows our sin and points out our depravity. The Apostles' Creed and Lord's Prayer are taught next to proclaim the good news that Christ has accomplished what the law requires, thereby saving us from our sin. In other words, the catechism presents to us law and Gospel.

Holy Scripture demonstrates the importance that fathers, or the head of the household, raise their children in the faith:

> *"Hear, O Israel: The LORD our God, the LORD is one. You shall love the LORD God with all your heart and with all your soul and with all your might. And these words that I command you today shall be on your heart.* **You shall teach them diligently to your children, and shall talk of them when you sit in your house, and when you walk by the way, and when you lie down, and when you rise.***"*

— *Deuteronomy 6:4-7* (ESV)

> *"Fathers, do not provoke your children to anger, but* **bring them up in the discipline and instruction of the Lord.***"*

— *Ephesians 56:4* (ESV)

> **"Train up a child in the way he should go**; *even when he is old he will not depart from it."*

— *Proverbs 2:6* (ESV)

At first glance, the classic *Book of Common Prayer* may appear to rest the responsibility of catechesis on the church, but let's reexamine the wording of the relevant rubric more carefully:

> *"And all Fathers, Mothers, Masters, and Mistresses,* **shall cause** *their Children, Servants, and Apprentices,* **who have not learned their Catechism***, to come to the Church at the time appointed, and obediently to hear and to be ordered by the Minister, until such time as they have learned all that is here appointed for them to learn."*

The requirement that children learn from the local minister is not a universal command but is contingent on those who have failed to memorize and understand the contents of the prayer book catechism. When the father or head of household neglect their duty to catechize their children, only then are they are required to send their children to the church to be taught the catechism by the resident minster. This implies that the preferred and expected scenario is one in which the father has taught his children the catechism.

Unfortunately, many Christian parents neglect their duty to God, the church, and their own children by failing to teach them the faith. The *Book of Common Prayer*'s catechism can and should be used by families to train their children to become disciples of Christ. Additionally, the 1928 U.S. *Book of Common Prayer* contains several flexible and easy-to-use condensed daily offices to teach doctrine, encourage

Bible reading, and teach the faith. This section is known as the "Forms of Prayer to be used in Families" at pages 587-600 of the 1928 *Book of Common Prayer*. It is this very section that is being expanded upon in this edited work of Bishop Edmund Gibson's prayers in Part Two, the "Family Devotions" section of this book.

Reviewing the catechism provides a solid Biblical and theological foundation for children. Additionally, teaching the catechism ensures that the children can be confirmed as members of the church and begin receiving Holy Communion. The catechesis of children provides them with a library of information they can rely upon as they grow in faith. Likewise, when asked about their faith, such as "what is a sacrament," they will have a ready answer: "an outward and visible sign of an inward and spiritual grace given unto us; ordained by Christ himself, as a means whereby we receive the same, and a pledge to assure us thereof." In theory, they will be able to draw upon the wisdom of the church and have an answer regarding the basic facts of Christianity.

Teaching the catechism can be tailored to suit a child's age and learning level. A great start is to begin with regular family prayer and including the memorization of one of the Ten Commandments, reciting the Apostles' Creed, and praying the Lord's Prayer. Over time, the Ten Commandments will be memorized, also with the Creed and Lord's Prayer becoming second nature. After learning the Ten Commandments, the Creed and Lord's Prayer provide more than enough material to review in detail. Parents can spend time teaching their children to learn the Lord's Prayer and Apostles' Creed line by line. The bite-size theology within the Creed and Lord's Prayer can easily be expanded upon when explaining to children, much less adults. It is very easy to spend a day or two discussing a single line from the Apostles' Creed or Lord's Prayer. Eventually, the theological meat of the rest of the catechism can be broached as children advance to school-age and after they have memorized the Ten Commandments, Apostles' Creed, and Lord's Prayer.

It is our duty to discipline, or disciple, our children in our faith. If we truly believe that God has revealed His love for us sinners through His Son, then we not only need to share this good news but raise our children to know and understand these facts. The catechism is not merely a tool to disciple our children but also a requirement for those of us within Anglicanism to know by heart. As parents, we would not fail to educate our children as to hygiene, nutrition, or the sciences. Why then should we neglect to teach them the riches, depth, and joy of God's mercy in providing for our salvation and the redemption of the world?

The Need for Common Prayer and Family Oratories

"Now you are the body of Christ and individually members of it."

- 1 *Corinthians* 12:27 (ESV)

American Christianity has embraced the zeitgeist of her culture and projects the individual as the ultimate unit in society much to the detriment of the family. While Christ came to save sinners, he also has called and elected his people to be built into His body, His temple. *See* 1 Peter 2:4-5, 9 ("As you come to him, a living stone rejected by men but in the sight of God chosen and precious, you yourselves like living stones are being built up as a spiritual house, to be a holy priesthood, to offer spiritual sacrifices acceptable to God through Jesus Christ. … But you are a chosen race, a royal priesthood, a holy nation, a people for his own possession, that you may proclaim the excellencies of him who called you out of darkness into his marvelous light.") (ESV).

The cell is the fundamental unit of the body, but individually cannot form tissue, organs, and parts of the body without working together with other cells. We are not called to be individual cells, but to work together and to become parts of the body of Christ. Furthermore, once joined with other cells (Christians) to form a part of the body (a family), we are to again come together corporately as the church with all parts of the body of Christ and to be united:

> For just as the body is one and has many members, and all the members of the body, though many, are one body, so it is with Christ. For in one Spirit we were all baptized into one body—Jews or Greeks, slaves or free—and all were made to drink of one Spirit. For the body does not consist of one member but of many. If the foot should say, "Because I am not a hand, I do not belong to the body," that would not make it any less a part of the body. And if the ear should say, "Because I am not an eye, I do not belong to the body," that would not make it any less a part of the body. If the whole body were an eye, where would be the sense of hearing? If the whole body were an ear, where would be the sense of smell? But as it is, God arranged the members in the body, each one of them, as he chose. If all were a single member, where would the body be? As it is, there are many parts, yet one body.

– 1 *Corinthians* 12:12-20 (ESV).

Families are traditionally the base unit and structure of the Christian church as they are the church-within-a-church and are the first unit of individual cells gathered together. Therefore, it is crucial that family prayer not only occur, but also catechesis (teaching) occur so that the children in families understand what the faith is and why we believe in Christ's atoning sacrifice and victorious resurrection. Only by being shaped by the waves of daily prayer and catechesis can one's mind be transformed so that our lives conform to the love that only the Spirit produces over and against the carnal self we are all born into.

Unfortunately, the American church is commonly a place for programs, seminars, and frankly worship that appeals to the individual and does not create a united body that the church is called to be. Instead, one may peruse a cafeteria of options of groups to attend, programs to participate in, and worship that suits one's personal tastes. Ironically, contemporary evangelicalism is appealing to many of the passions and desires of the old man, without any formation of church members into becoming transformed and transforming Christians. At the end of the day, the American church is creating a creed-less Christian (an oxymoron) whose loyalty to his church is solely based upon what appeals to him, and not any underlying objective truth taught by the church through catechesis, confession, and creed. It is a Christianity set adrift with no firm anchor or foundation. It is a building made of straw on sand and will not stand when challenged but will remain popular because it appeals to self instead of worshiping the Creator beyond us. In effect, our personal tastes are what we worship, and we become our own idol.

This is why the *Book of Common Prayer* is what American Christianity needs. It provides a standard of doctrine reflecting a broad orthodoxy of Reformed thought during the early Reformation and provides a manner of prayers rooted in Trinitarian worship and focused on family use for building up the body of Christ. It provides a rule, or discipline, that has been simplified from the dedicated Benedictine Order. This rule of prayer is the rule of our belief and ultimately the rule of how we live (*lex orandi, lex credendi, lex vivendi*). In other words, the prayers presented by the *Book of Common Prayer* in Morning and Evening Prayer shapes our faith through the wording of the services. Additionally, the services of Morning and Evening Prayer provide not only a set of prayers and optional prayers but calls for a daily recitation of the Apostles' Creed, the Lord's Prayer, and selections from the Bible. When regularly performed, one will quickly learn the Creed, Lord's Prayer, and other prayers by heart to reflect upon and pray throughout the day. Additionally, the lectionary allows for one to essentially read the entire Bible within a year (when using the 1662 lectionary). When such a discipline of regular prayer is adopted not only by the individual, but also by the family, it naturally builds up a unit of cells within the greater body of Christ.

How can Christians be built up into stronger units of the body of Christ? Through prayer, catechesis, and ultimately living out the faith through service to our neighbor. This is what inspired my own family to begin a family oratory and to open it to other families. We base our prayer life through the *Book of Common Prayer* not out of Anglican superiority, but because we are biblical and catholic Christians and believe that our prayer book provides a broad reformed and catholic orthodoxy that bridges the divide between Lutherans and Reformed Christians. Additionally, in a time and place where the majority of American Christians are in a non-liturgical, non-creedal, and un-catechized church, the creation of family oratories serve as beacons and networks of light for many American Christians who do not realize the depth of our faith, much less fundamental doctrines every layman should know.

Being the body of Christ is not traversing one church program to the next but is a discipline that creates disciples who go out into the world. Until we know our faith through catechism, conform our lives to daily prayer, and let those prayers transform us into actively obeying Christ through serving others, we are merely pagans wearing Christian makeup.

Every Home a Chapel Common Prayer in Practice

It is important that families pray together as the basic building block upon which the Church is built upon. To that effect, the 1928 *Book of Common Prayer* at p. 587 provides a form for Morning and Evening Prayer that is shortened from the regular and more formal daily office. Additionally, an even shorter form of both Morning and Evening Prayer are provided for busy families starting on p. 592. Finally, a selection of Additional Prayers are included at p. 594 that can be used as appropriate during a family gathering for daily prayer or separately when applicable to a situation. Of course, there are also the additional Prayers and Thanksgivings located after the full office of Evening Prayer starting at p. 35.

These tools are useful in assisting families seeking to pray regularly together. The purpose is not to merely recite one or both offices daily for the sake of checking it off of a spiritual to-do list but to be used as a tool in discipling families. The regular use of the daily offices is a discipline that easily catechizes the family to quickly learn the Lord's Prayer, especially for the youngest members of the family. Including the readings from the 1662 lectionary will ensure the Word of God is taught by hearing and will result in nearly the entire Bible being heard through a single year.

As children come of age, one can easily incorporate elements of the Catechism that begins just prior to the

Family Prayer section in preparation for their Confirmation into the church. Additionally, the Thirty-Nine Articles are conveniently located just after the Family Prayer section in the 1928 *Book of Common Prayer* and can be referenced as needed for answering and teaching the reformed catholicism that embodies the Anglican faith.

The prior chapter mentioned expanding family oratories into something more – what was once referred to as a religious society. A religious society would consist of families gathered to recite a daily office and reading from the lectionary. In common parlance, a "small group." Such a gathering of several families together as a small group could consist of reciting Evening Prayer (using the shorter versions in the *Book of Common Prayer* Family Prayer section considering the presence of small children who will likely have a difficult time remaining attentive for a full Evening Prayer service). However, for those families with older children, the full Evening Prayer service can be recited by the laity, minus the absolution after the confession of sins (only an ordained presbyter, or priest, is allowed to pronounce the absolution), under thirty minutes.

Creating a small group of families committed to a rule of weekly prayer is easy enough. Start small with a shorter Evening Prayer service from the Family Prayer section and perhaps only meet once a month at first with another family (the meeting location can swap to make it easier on the families participating and to avoid a regular host family from being "burned out"). The evening could start with a small potluck dinner and after blessing the meal the relevant biblical texts from the lectionary could be read and reflected upon over dinner (a modern adaptation of the *agape* feast, *see* Jude 1:12). Afterwards, the host family could lead the group in the Evening Prayer service. Eventually, portions of the catechism can be added after Evening Prayer, with a focus on the young children learning the responses in preparation for their confirmation. For older children and the adults, the Thirty-Nine Articles of Religion can be read and discussed as they relate to what was discussed regarding the church catechism or lectionary readings.

Naturally, young children will want to be busybodies and play but the fact they hear the daily office being read week after week will soak into them. What is important is that they see their parents taking the obligation of prayer and Bible reading seriously. Over time, the children will learn the Lord's Prayer and Apostles' Creed by "osmosis." I say this from personal experience in merely being raised a regular Sunday churchgoer in the United Methodist Church, where I easily learned the Lord's Prayer and Apostles' Creed by heart at a very young age simply from attending the services regularly. I will forever be grateful that my local United Methodist Church congregation had not (yet) abandoned the traditional language and outline of a *Book of Common Prayer* service. Now, as a father of two I am seeing my own children learning the prayers of the church after regularly attending services and participating in our family prayers.

The 1928 *Book of Common Prayer*'s Catechism and Office of Instruction are both very elementary and short documents within the prayer book that are useful in learning the faith. Additionally, the Thirty-Nine Articles of Religion can be quickly read throughout the course of several weeks (although one could easily spend years on the Thirty-Nine Articles – they are short but theologically a deep well). Once a family network/small group exhausts studying these resources, a printed homily or reading from a church father could replace the catechism and Thirty-Nine Articles to enrich and educate attendees on the meaning of the lectionary text associated with the Evening Prayer daily office. Additionally, the small group could read through selections from the two Books of Homilies, or at least the homily "Of the Salvation of all Mankind" (which is specifically referenced as the "Homily of Justification" by Article XI of the Thirty-Nine Articles). With the internet at one's fingertips there are a plethora of free sources of classic sermons, catechisms, and commentaries.

Essentially, if a couple of families (or more) are willing to gather regularly and pray a daily office I suggest they begin with a meal and discussing the relevant Bible readings and then flow into a short Evening Prayer service. I encourage families to press on and do a short reading and discussion of the catechism and Thirty-Nine Articles when one is starting their fellowship of families so that everyone is, in theory, will be well-grounded on the basics of the Trinitarian and orthodox Christian faith.

The key to such a fellowship is to find a few like-minded persons who are committed praying together and seeking holiness in the day-to-day. The first several meetings will be awkward in execution but persevere and things will begin to flow more naturally. Starting off slowly is better than trying to go "all-in" initially. A meal where everyone alternates reading the lectionary texts and then engage in a short form of Evening Prayer is an excellent start to hopefully something that will grow into the full daily office and deeper theological study over time.

Catechesis through Singing

Advent, the season of the year in which singing resurges in religious and secular homes alike. Songs such as "O Come, O Come Emmanuel", "Joy to the World" (yes, it is an Advent hymn), and "O Holy Night" (okay, a Christmas hymn) are staples this season of the year. They are easily memorable tunes and verses. Additionally, these songs are chock-full of incarnational and Trinitarian theology that can be reflected upon while singing.

Singing hymns with the family is immensely more fun for young children than teaching the catechism (at least in my experience!) and results in quicker memorization. Granted, the deep riches of the verses of these songs and the meaning of the words may not be fully grasped by young children, but learning these songs will provide foundational doctrine that can be drawn upon at a moment's notice. My own understanding of the incarnation has been enriched through the verses of traditional Christian hymnody. Singing hymns can capture one's heart in a manner that reading simply cannot. There is beauty in poetry, and the Bible is full of poetry that can be sung, such as the Psalter.

Teaching children classic hymns provides them songs directing them towards Christ and His work. It is a natural educational tool for younger kids to draw upon. Since my daughter was at the tender age of three, she regularly belts out the classic African-American spiritual, "Go Tell it on the Mountain" and is excited to select hymns to sing from our family hymnal. She has even surprised me in learning how to sing the Latin to "Angels We Have Heard on High," as she belts out the chorus, which states in part, "Gloria, in excelsis Deo!" It brings her such joy to sing hymns and she regularly asks to see the family hymnal and flip through its pages while singing (the song she thinks) is on the page. Another added benefit is she now wants to participate more in Sunday worship as the pew hymnal is familiar to her.

Although she has not learned a whole hymn to sing by heart, she can join in at various portions of several songs. Additionally, during our evening devotion we discuss a verse and its meaning to explain the hymn we sing that night. Discussing a hymn's content quickly becomes a lesson on why the wise men traveled to see Jesus and present Him gifts or why Christ is called Emmanuel.

On a similar note, I commend the Reformed Episcopal Church (REC) in their new hymnal, the Book of Common Praise, for including several annotated sections of the *Book of Common Prayer*. It would be wise for families (and Anglican churches) to sing portions of the prayer book to assist in teaching the words of the Psalter, the canticles, and the services to their children through singing. Indeed, it is a long-term goal of mine to incorporate Anglican chant into our family devotions. Notably, REC's Book of Common Praise includes a short section on Anglican chant – a noteworthy addition that I greatly value and appreciate.

Practically speaking, I encourage families to begin with simple, short songs for their very young children. We began with "Jesus Loves Me" and eventually progressed to more familiar traditional hymns, typically Advent and Christmas themed due to my own familiarity with songs from those seasons. There is no right or wrong way to begin such a practice – just dive in!

Our custom is to sing one or two songs, share a Biblical story or parable of Christ, and conclude with the Lord's Prayer and/or Apostles' Creed. As an Anglican, I use this pattern in order for my children to learn the requirements for confirmation: the Creed, Ten Commandments, Lord's Prayer, and eventually the catechism. *See* 1928 *Book of Common Prayer*, Rubric at end of Office of Instruction. This pattern is easily amendable to Trinitarian Christians across the theological spectrum of Protestant, Eastern Orthodox, or Roman Catholic. Start early with your children no matter their age. Remember starting today is better than waiting until tomorrow. Family devotionals are messy, but necessary to build up catechized and well-discipled members of the Church.

Reformation, Authority, Anglicanism, and the Home Oratory

On the eve[5] of the 500th anniversary of Luther's Ninety-five Theses, we face the same question the Augustinian monk faced: authority. Be it a pope releasing a papal bull in the Vatican or a Baptist pronouncing truth as though he were the pope, Christians face the same question as to who, or what, is authoritative in the Christian life.

The Reformers answered the question by pointing to Scripture as **the** primary authority. The English Reformation agreed that as it pertains to matters of salvation, *sola scriptura* wins the day. (Art. VI of the Thirty-Nine Articles of Religion). The tradition of the church and church fathers were not discarded, as one can plainly read in the writings of the magisterial reformers and in the numerous citations to the church fathers in the Anglican two Books of Homilies. Instead, the Reformers set the writings of the church fathers beneath the Scriptures to ensure that authority started and rested with the Word of God.

Unfortunately, contemporary Protestantism has forgotten the works of the Reformers and their actual teachings. Protestants today are typically more likely to read Scripture and interpret it as they subjectively feel and without any guidance of the church, much less ancient church fathers. Shockingly, many denominations and their followers, have not the

---

[5] This was originally written in 2017.

slightest idea about the confessions the Reformers subscribed to that detail their reformed or reforming Catholicism.

However, not everyone in Protestant circles have forgotten that Protestantism, at its best, is a reformed Catholic religion. The *Reforming Catholic Confession*[6] is an effort to demonstrate the highest common denominator of Protestant catholicity and is an effort to be commended, although certainly not a perfect exercise.

The lack of authority and trading in one pope in the Vatican for a dozen in every Bible study is not a uniquely Protestant problem, but a modern one. The Bible study (or Christian denomination) that trades objective truth for "my truth" or "this is how I read/understand this passage" is not what the Reformers had in mind. This stereotype serves as cannon fodder for Eastern Orthodox and Roman Catholic polemics (which ignores that the same problem infects both of those churches as well – this is a modern issue that does not limit itself to Protestant circles).

Indeed, the Anglican Communion has lost her way in failing to hold to an authority that transcends the globe and unite multiple national churches behind a common belief. In the spirit of the 500th anniversary of Luther's Ninety-five Theses, the Anglican churches and her members must remember what unites them as

---

[6] The text is available at https://reformingcatholicconfession.com/.

Anglicans. In order to do so, Anglicans must remember what makes them Anglican.

Ultimately, the basis of our rule of faith is the Holy Scriptures, with the Apocrypha included for the edification of the Christian but not as a source for doctrine. This decision to include the Apocrypha as useful instruction but not for determining doctrine firmly lies rooted within church history and relying on the church fathers. Article VI of the Thirty-Nine Articles of Religion cite St. Jerome for this proposition. The ultimate rule as to our salvation comes from Scripture alone. But what if the Scriptures are silent? Article XX explains that the church has the authority to determine rites and ceremonies in addition to determining controversies, but the church must never contradict the ultimate authority of Holy Scripture.

Anglicans have another guide to walking and living life as reformed Catholics, namely the Thirty-Nine Articles of Religion. They have been tossed aside to small print and behind the section "Historical Documents" in the 1979 *Book of Common Prayer* or used as a weapon by those with Genevan sympathies to erect a hardline Calvinism. But the Thirty-Nine Articles are a work of genius that were enacted in the Elizabethan settlement and walk in and out of the theologies of Geneva (Calvin) and Wittenberg (Luther) with a solid foothold on historic catholic teaching. I dare say the Thirty-Nine Articles embody the essence of a reformed Catholicism with the insight of Luther, Calvin, and historic Christianity both Eastern and Western. The

Thirty-Nine Articles does this all the while without throwing any babies out of the bathwater.

The old saying is the rule of prayer is the rule of belief: *lex orandi, lex credendi*. Enter the next guideline for Anglicans, the *Book of Common Prayer*. The classical prayer book serves as the source for public worship for reformed Catholics in the Anglican tradition. The abbreviated daily offices (from seven to two offices) allow the laity to worship in a manner similar to the Rule of St. Benedict. The Eucharist is restored to the laity and encouraged to be performed often. And the Ordinal attached is the defining fence post for church leadership and the role of ordained minsters.

Fortunately, the three "guideposts" defining Anglicanism: the *Book of Common Prayer*, Thirty-Nine Articles, and Ordinal are all included within published versions of the *Book of Common Prayer*. One can even purchase the Holy Scriptures (with Apocrypha) and 1928 American *Book of Common Prayer* (with Thirty-Nine Articles and the Ordinal) in one bound volume.[7]

As it relates to family oratories, the primary authority of Scripture, followed by the guidance of the *Book of Common Prayer*, Thirty-Nine Articles, and the Ordinal serve as the backbone of practicing reformed Catholicism in the home. The 1928 American, 2003 REC, and to a lesser extent the 2019 ACNA *Book of Common Prayer*, also have the benefit of including family

---

[7] The Anglican Parishes Association Publications sells these online at https://anglican-parishes-association.myshopify.com/.

prayers to guide family praise, worship, and petitions. Additionally, the historic prayer book catechism provides a succinct overview of the Christian faith and life easily digestible for children and adults alike.

Singing can also be accomplished through singing the Psalter included in the *Book of Common Prayer*. Since plainsong, chant, or metrical tune is rare, the authorized hymnal can provide the source for singing in a family context. Indeed, hymnals with theologically rich songs serve as a lesser authority to the Anglican formularies outlined earlier, but nevertheless can support the mission of an oratory to disciple children and adults in the faith.

Finally, a forgotten "semi-guidepost," are the two Books of Homilies. These sermons were officially written by the Church of England and although several are dated, can still be useful in the home for teaching and are useful for laity in understanding the church's doctrine. Although not on the same level as the *Book of Common Prayer* and Articles of Religion, Article XI cites directly to one of the homilies for a deeper understanding of the official position for Anglicans on justification by faith. This homily ("Of the Salvation of Mankind," but cited as the "Homily of Justification" in Article XI) refutes the typical polemic that Anglicans reject good works by explaining succinctly:

> *Faith alone, how it is to be understood. Nevertheless, this sentence, that we be justified by faith only, is not so*

meant of them, that the said justifying faith is alone in man, without true repentance, hope, charity, dread, and the fear of GOD, at any time and season. Nor when they say, That we be justified freely, they mean not that we should or might afterward be idle, and that nothing should be required on our parts afterward: Neither they mean not so to be justified without good works, that we should do no good works at all, like as shall be more expressed at large hereafter. But this saying, That we be justified by faith only, freely and without works, is spoken for to take away clearly all merit of our works, as being unable to deserve our justification at GODS hands, and thereby most plainly to express the weakness of man, and the goodness of GOD, the great infirmity of our selves, and the might and power of GOD, the imperfectness of our own works, and the most abundant grace of our Savior Christ, and therefore wholly to ascribe the merit and deserving of our justification unto Christ only, and his most precious blood shedding.

<u>*They that continue in evil living, have not true faith.*</u>
For how can a man have this true faith, this sure trust and confidence in GOD, that by the merits of Christ, his sins be forgiven, and be reconciled to the favor of GOD, and to be partaker of the kingdom of heaven by Christ, when he lives ungodly, and denies Christ in his deeds? Surely no such ungodly man can have this faith and trust in GOD. For as they know Christ to be the only savior of the world: so they know also that wicked men shall not enjoy the kingdom of GOD. They know that GOD hates unrighteousness (Psalms 5.5-6), that he will destroy all those that speak untruly, that those which have done good works (which cannot be done

> *without a lively faith in Christ) shall come forth into the resurrection of life, and those that have done evil, shall come unto the resurrection of judgement: very well they know also, that to them that be contentious, and to them that will not be obedient unto the truth, but will obey unrighteousness, shall come indignation, wrath, and affliction, &c.*[8]

The bottom line is a Christian must be governed and rooted in an authority, the question is who or what? Although contemporary Protestantism, Anglicanism, and frankly Christians of all persuasions have deviated to following what they subjectively "feel" is true, this ignores the objective guideposts that fence-in the beliefs of reformed Catholics. Families seeking such a guidepost for their own discipleship should look to the Anglican path as one that provides a number of resources and tools that are reformed **and** catholic in the best sense of both words, and both worlds. Let us pick up the prayer book, learn its prayers, breathe its doctrine, and be formed by its confession of the faith once delivered to the saints.

---

[8] I highly suggest Dr. Gerald Bray's *The Book of Homilies: A Critical Edition*, James Clarke & Co. (2017) for those in the market for the two Books of Homilies.

The Home as a Monastery

Life is fairly repetitive for the average American, but this does not mean we can simply "check out" from following Christ and advancing His kingdom simply because we are overworked and tired. No, we should embrace the mundane in our life and use it for opportunity to grow as Christians. The woman trapped in her cubicle or parent who is rocking his child at 3am is doing something holy. They are participating in their vocation to the glory of God.

We should contemplate the work we have immediately before us and remind ourselves that what we do can be done either as an act of worship or as an act of my own sinful self. Take household chores for example. I could begrudgingly and under protest take out the trash all the while bemoaning the fact to my spouse, or I could simply do the task and use the time to pray the Lord's Prayer – an act of love to my neighbor, my wife, and an act of love to God, by obeying Christ's command to pray the Lord's Prayer.

As a husband, my cell is my work office and my ministry extends from phone calls and work meetings to demonstrating my love for my wife by and through taking on chores without her request. Further, we have not only a rule of life: love thy neighbor or spouse or children through your acts; but also a rule of prayer as evidenced by the *Book of Common Prayer*. Engaging in regular family prayer is the rule of prayer in our quaint abbey, also known as our home.

Beyond regular prayer and engaging in the work needed to run the household, our household should regularly gather (preferably over a meal) to give thanks to God for His blessings and to sing praises in the form of a hymn or Psalm to His Holy Name. Finally, celebrating Saint's Days and other feasts of the church assists in reminding our children and ourselves that the kingdom of God is among us, near us, and within us. Such celebrations remind us that liturgically, we are on God's time and not the world's schedule. Likewise, it raises children to expect not only seasons of the year but also feast days of the year and to remind ourselves that we are a part of the wider "communion of saints" who have gone before us. Additionally, denying yourself during fasts keeps in mind that we do not belong to ourself, but belong to God. And we were saved by Him to perform good works for our neighbor. When you fast as a family, you build a common bond and identity in Christ.

Every home has its own abbot or abbess, namely the father and mother. And we are responsible like any good abbot or abbess for the monks in our care, namely our children. Therefore, let us strive to raise little monks who know their faith and who know the Scriptures by heart, can recite the Lord's Prayer and Apostles' Creed, and answer the church catechism. For at the end of this age, we must give an account for what we have done and what we have left undone. We have promised to raise our children before God's church and at their baptism to raise them in the faith.

We must now get to work in teaching our children, and what better way than through family prayer and devotions?

Part Two

FAMILY DEVOTIONS

The following is the edited Family Daily Offices and selection of prayers for all occasions originally authored by Bishop Edmund Gibson for the Diocese of London. I have minimally edited the language to assist in your own family devotions.

FAMILY OFFICE
MORNING PRAYER

¶ The head of the household having called together the Family says the following with all kneeling, with all repeating the Lord's Prayer:

Let us pray:

OUR Father, who art in heaven, Hallowed be thy Name. Thy kingdom come. Thy will be done, On earth as it is in heaven. Give us this day our daily bread. And forgive us our trespasses, As we forgive those who trespass against us. And lead us not into temptation, But deliver us from evil. For thine is the kingdom, and the power, and the glory, for ever and ever. Amen.

¶ Here may follow the Collect for the day.
¶ Here may follow the Daily Lectionary reading of the Psalter, read responsively.
¶ Here may follow the Daily Lectionary reading from the Old and New Testaments.

Acknowledgment of God's Mercy and Preservation through the Night

ALMIGHTY and everlasting God, in Whom we live, move, have our life, and whose mercy is all over Your works; We, your needy creatures, give You our humble praises, for our preservation from the beginning of our lives to this day. Blessed be Your holy Name for the continued protection by Your hand, by which we have been and delivered from the dangers of the past night. By You we are brought in safety to the beginning of this day. For your mercies, we bless and magnify your glorious Name; asking you to accept this our morning sacrifice of praise and thanksgiving; for the sake Him who lay down in the grave, and rose again for us, your Son our Savior Jesus Christ. *Amen.*

Dedication of Soul and Body to God's Service

Since it is of your mercy gracious Father that another day is added to our lives; We here dedicate both our souls and our bodies to Your service, for a sober, righteous, and godly life. We renounce the devil and all his works, the vanities of this evil age, and all the sinful lusts of the flesh; desiring nothing so much as to serve You faithfully all the days of our lives. Sincerely we resolve to improve, and each day become better servants of You and persevere in holiness and righteousness until the end. We ask You merciful God to confirm and strengthen us; that, as we grow in age, we may grow in grace, and in the knowledge of our Lord and Savior Jesus Christ. *Amen.*

But God, who knows the weakness and corruption of our nature, and the many temptations which we daily meet; We humbly ask You to have compassion on our weaknesses, and to give us the constant assistance of Your Holy Spirit; that we may be restrained from sin, and reminded of our duty to You. When You see us giving into temptation, prevent us from being tempted beyond our ability, and stretch out Your helping hand to save and deliver us.

Imprint upon our hearts such a dread of your judgments, and such a grateful sense of your goodness to us, as may make us both afraid and ashamed to offend You. And, above all, remind us of that great day, in which we must give a strict account of our thoughts, words, and actions to Him whom you have appointed the Judge of quick and dead, your Son Jesus Christ our Lord. *Amen.*

¶ *Here may follow a hymn, canticle, or the Apostles' Creed*

For Grace to guide and keep us the following Day, and for God's Blessing

So we may give a good account of today, give us grace to have You and your holy Law before our eyes, that we may walk in it according to Your will and guidance. We implore Your grace and protection for the ensuing day. Keep us sober and moderate in all things, including food and drink, and diligent in our several callings and vocations which Your Providence has appointed us. Grant us patience under our afflictions and minds always content with our present condition. Give us grace to be just and upright in all our dealings; peaceable among our neighbors; compassionate towards the needy and afflicted; and ready to do good to all, according to our abilities and opportunities. Through walking faithfully before You throughout our days, and being found watchful for our appointed time, we may from a life of righteousness be translated to a life of glory, through the merits and mediation of Jesus Christ, our only Savior and Redeemer. *Amen.*

For God's blessing upon the business of the day

Now we are entering upon the work of the vocations which Your Providence has placed us, and we truly ask Your blessing this day upon our plans and work ahead. Direct us in all our ways and prosper the works of our hands.

We desire to walk in a constant sense of Your all-seeing Providence, therefore preserve our coming and going throughout this day. Defend us from all dangers and adversities; and be pleased to take us, and our dear loved ones, under your fatherly care and protection. These things, and whatever You see necessary for us, we humbly ask You, through the merits and mediation of your Son Jesus Christ, our Lord and Savior. *Amen.*

On Sunday mornings, say:

As we go to public worship, we ask you to let Your Holy Spirit accompany us, and make us devout, serious and attentive, raise our minds from the thoughts of this world to the consideration of the next, that we fervently join in the prayers and praises of Your church, and listen to our duty with honest hearts, in order to practice it. And give us grace to dedicate this day, as You have appointed us, to Your service and the care of our souls. Direct us in all our ways and guide our feet into Your paths. *Amen.*

The grace of our Lord Jesus Christ, and the love of God, and the fellowship of the Holy Spirit, be with us all evermore. *Amen.*

FAMILY OFFICE
EVENING PRAYER

¶ The head of household with all the Family kneeling, and repeating with him the Lord's Prayer

Let us pray:

OUR Father, who art in heaven, Hallowed be thy Name. Thy kingdom come. Thy will be done, On earth as it is in heaven. Give us this day our daily bread. And forgive us our trespasses, As we forgive those who trespass against us. And lead us not into temptation, But deliver us from evil. For thine is the kingdom, and the power, and the glory, for ever and ever. Amen.

¶ Here may follow the Collect for the day
¶ Here may follow the Daily Lectionary reading of the Psalter, read responsively
¶ Here may follow the Daily Lectionary reading from the Old and New Testaments

Confession of Sins, with a Prayer for Contrition and Pardon

Let us silently confess our sins before Almighty God.

MOST gracious and merciful God, who are of purer eyes than to behold iniquity, and has promised mercy and forgiveness to all those who confess and forsake their sins; We come before You in a humble sense of our own unworthiness, acknowledging our many transgressions of your righteous laws, in thought, word, and deed. We have every day done those things which You have forbidden, and left undone the things which You have commanded. When we look upon our past lives and remember that You know our most secret sins, we are afraid of Your judgments and are ashamed to lift up our eyes to You.

* Here let him who reads make a short pause, that everyone may secretly confess the sins and failings of that day.

* But, O gracious Father, who desire not the death of a sinner, look upon us as we ask you to be merciful through Your Son, Jesus Christ, for the merits of His sufferings, and forgive us all our transgressions. Make us deeply aware of the great evil of them; and work within us a broken and contrite heart leading to a lamentation of our sins and a holy repentance; that we may obtain forgiveness at Your hands, Who always is ready to receive humble and penitent sinners; for the sake of Your Son Jesus Christ, our only Savior and Redeemer. *Amen.*

Prayer for Grace to reform and grow better

And prior to succumbing to our own frailty, or the temptations which encompass us, or we are drawn again into sin, protect us through the direction and assistance of your Holy Spirit. Reform whatever is amiss within our souls; that no unclean thoughts, unlawful designs, or wrongful desires, may rest there. Purge our hearts from envy, hatred, and malice; that we may never allow the sun to go down upon our anger; but may always go to our rest in peace, charity, and good-will, with a conscience void of offence towards you, and towards all so that so our hearts are fit for Your Holy Spirit's dwelling and whether we wake or sleep, will be under His blessed protection, and have our whole spirit, soul, and body preserved pure and blameless, unto the coming of our Lord and Savior Jesus Christ. *Amen.*

The Intercession

Accept O Lord as evidence of our love and charity, our intercessions for all mankind. Let the light of your Gospel shine upon all nations; and may as many as have received it, live renewed lives. Be gracious unto Your Church; and grant that every member of the same, in their vocation and ministry, may serve you faithfully. Bless all in authority over us; and so rule their hearts and strengthen their hands, that they may punish wickedness and maintain your true religion and virtue. Send down your blessings, temporal and spiritual, upon all our family, friends, and neighbors. Reward all who have done us good, and pardon all those who have done or wish us evil, and give them repentance and better minds. Be merciful to all who are in any trouble and affliction of mind or body; and do administer to them according to their needs; for the sake of He who went about doing good to the souls and bodies of men, Your Son our Savior Jesus Christ. *Amen.*

¶ Here may follow a hymn, canticle, or Apostles' Creed

The Thanksgiving

To our prayers, O Lord, we join our sincere thanks for all your mercies; our life, our reason, and all other gifts of soul and body. We thank you Lord for our health, friends, food, clothing, and all the other comforts and conveniences of life. Above all, we adore Your mercy in sending Your only Son into the world, to redeem us from sin and eternal death, and in giving us the knowledge and sense of our duty towards You. We bless You for your patience with us, notwithstanding our many and great sins. We bless You for all the directions, assistance, and comforts of Your Holy Spirit; for Your continual care and watchful Providence over us through the whole course of our lives; and particularly for the mercies and benefits of the past day. We humbly ask you to continue your blessings to us, and to give us grace to show our thankfulness in a sincere obedience to Your laws, through whose merits and intercession we received them, Your Son our Savior Jesus Christ. *Amen.*

Prayer for God's Protection through the Night following

In particular, we ask you to continue your gracious protection to us this night. Defend us from all dangers and from fear that we may enjoy refreshing sleep for the duties of the coming day. And grant us grace always to live in such a manner that we may never be afraid to die; so that, living and dying, we may be Yours through the merits and satisfaction of Your Son Christ Jesus, in whose Name we offer up these our imperfect prayers. *Amen.*

The grace of our Lord Jesus Christ, and the love of God, and the fellowship of the Holy Spirit, be with us all evermore. *Amen.*

A SHORTER FORM OF THE FAMILY DAILY OFFICES
MORNING

¶ After the reading of a brief portion of Holy Scripture, let the Head of the Household, or some other member of the family, say as follows with all kneeling, and repeating with him the Lord's Prayer.

OUR Father, who art in heaven, Hallowed be thy Name. Thy kingdom come. Thy will be done, On earth as it is in heaven. Give us this day our daily bread. And forgive us our trespasses, As we forgive those who trespass against us. And lead us not into temptation, But deliver us from evil. For thine is the kingdom, and the power, and the glory, for ever and ever. Amen.

LORD, our heavenly Father, Almighty and everlasting God, Who has safely brought us to the beginning of this day; please defend us with Your mighty power; and grant that this day we not fall into sin, neither run into any kind of danger; but that all our doings, being ordered by Your governance, may be righteous in your sight; through Jesus Christ our Lord. *Amen.*

¶ Here may be added any special Prayers.

The grace of our Lord Jesus Christ, and the love of God, and the fellowship of the Holy Spirit, be with us all evermore. *Amen.*

A SHORTER FORM OF THE FAMILY DAILY OFFICES
EVENING

¶ After the reading of a brief portion of Holy Scripture, let the Head of the Household, or some other member of the family, say as follows with all kneeling and repeating with him the Lord's Prayer.

OUR Father, who art in heaven, Hallowed be thy Name. Thy kingdom come. Thy will be done, On earth as it is in heaven. Give us this day our daily bread. And forgive us our trespasses, As we forgive those who trespass against us. And lead us not into temptation, But deliver us from evil. For thine is the kingdom, and the power, and the glory, for ever and ever. Amen.

Enlighten our darkness, we beg you O Lord; and by Your great mercy defend us from all perils and dangers of this night; for the love of your only Son, our Savior, Jesus Christ. *Amen.*

¶ Here may be added any special Prayers

The Lord bless us and keep us. The Lord make his face to shine upon us, and be gracious unto us. The Lord lift up his countenance upon us, and give us peace, this night and evermore. *Amen.*

AN ORDER FOR PRIVATE INDIVIDUAL
MORNING PRAYER

¶ When you rise from bed in the morning, begin.

"I laid me down and slept, and rose up again, for the Lord sustained me." Psalm 3:5.

Almighty and Everlasting God, in Whom I live, move, and have my life, and whose mercy is all over Your works; I give you humble thanks for the preservation of my life. I thank You that You have protected me from the perils and dangers of the past night and have given me quiet and comfortable rest and brought me safely to the beginning of this day. Allow the same good Providence to continue to watch over me and preserve my comings and goings, that I may be defended from all dangers, the temptations of the world, the flesh, and the devil. Give me grace to act soberly, diligently, honestly, in my vocation, and with duty and submission to those You have set over me; and to desire and endeavor to live in peace and love with my neighbors. Preserve within me a strict regard to truth and sincerity in all my words and actions and let no fear of punishment or displeasure from men ever make me transgress my duty to You.

To the end may I walk in Your fear this day, and all the days of my life; keep in my mind a due sense and reverence of Your all-knowing wisdom, and the remembrance that in the last day I must give a strict account of my thoughts, words, and actions; and according to the works done in my body, be sentenced by Your righteous judgment for eternity. Grant this, O Father, for the sake of Your Son Jesus Christ, my blessed Savior and Redeemer. *Amen.*

AN ORDER FOR PRIVATE INDIVIDUAL
EVENING PRAYER

¶ *Just prior to entering your bed, begin.*

Most gracious God, who by Your wise Providence have appointed to Mankind several vocations and offices in this life, I acknowledge Your wisdom and goodness; You desire all things submit to Your holy will. To this end, provide me with a spirit of humility, patience, and contentment, as is suitable to the condition in which Your Providence has placed me. Bless me with good health, a comforted mind that I may perform my work with cheerfulness and doing my duty to You, and resting on the gracious promises for a reward of my labor and obedience in this life.

Since, through the frailty of my nature and the numerous temptations which I daily meet, I cannot always stand upright; I pray You to forgive me all transgressions of my duty, whether in thought, word, or deed, and especially forgive the sins and failings of the past day, and enable me through the Holy Spirit to avoid them for the future, and to be ever growing in the graces and virtues of the Christian life, as long as You shall be pleased to continue my life in this world. I thank You for your constant care over me considering the changes of this mortal life, and in particular for Your preservation of my life during this past day. I ask You to continue Your gracious protection to me this night that I may enjoy such quiet and refreshing sleep as may fit me for the duties of the next day. I ask you for this in the Name and for the merits of Your Son Jesus Christ, my blessed Savior and Redeemer. *Amen.*

OUR Father, who art in heaven; hallowed be thy Name. Thy kingdom come. Thy will be done, On earth as it is in Heaven. Give us this day our daily bread; and forgive us our trespasses, as we forgive those who trespass against us. And lead us not into temptation, but deliver us from evil. For thine is the kingdom, and the power, and the glory, forever and ever. *Amen.*

"I will lie me down in peace, and take my rest, for it is You, Lord, only, that makes me dwell in safety."
Psalm 4:9.

ADDITIONAL PRAYERS

For the Spirit of Prayer

ALMIGHTY God, who pours out on all who desires the spirit of grace and of prayer; Deliver us, when we draw away from you due to coldness of heart and wanderings of our mind so that with a diligent mind and heart we may worship You in spirit and in truth; through Jesus Christ our Lord. *Amen.*

In the Morning

O GOD, the King eternal, who separated the day from the night, and turns the shadow of death into the morning; Drive far off from us all wrong desires, incline our hearts to keep Your law, and guide our feet into the way of peace; that having done Your will with cheerfulness while it was day, we may, when the night arrives, rejoice to give You thanks; through Jesus Christ our Lord. *Amen.*

ALMIGHTY God, who alone provide us the breath of life, and alone can keep alive in us the holy desires you do provide; We ask You for your compassion's sake, to sanctify all our thoughts and endeavors; that we may neither begin an action without a pure intention nor continue it without Your blessing. And grant that, having the eyes of the mind opened to behold things invisible and unseen, we may in he be inspired by your wisdom, and in work be upheld by Your strength, and in the end be accepted by You as Your faithful servants; through Jesus Christ our Savior. *Amen.*

At Night

O LORD, support us all the day long, until the shadows lengthen and the evening comes, and the busy world is hushed, and the fever of life is over, and our work is done. Then in your mercy grant us a safe lodging, and a holy rest, and peace at the last. *Amen.*

O GOD, who are the life of mortal men, the light of the faithful, the strength of those who labor, and the repose of the dead; We thank you for the timely blessings of the day, and humbly ask for your merciful protection all this night. Bring us in safety to the morning hours; through Him who died for us and rose again, Your Son, our Savior Jesus Christ. *Amen.*

Sunday Morning

O GOD, who makes us glad with the weekly remembrance of the glorious resurrection of Your Son our Lord; Provide us this day such a blessing through our worship of you, that the days to come may be spent in Your service; through the same Jesus Christ our Lord. *Amen.*

For Quiet Confidence

O GOD of peace, who has taught us that in returning and rest we shall be saved, in quietness and in confidence shall be our strength; By the might of Your Spirit lift us, we pray for Your presence, where we may be still and know that You are God; through Jesus Christ our Lord. *Amen.*

For Guidance

O GOD, by whom the meek are guided in judgment, and light rises up in darkness for the godly; Grant us, in all our doubts and uncertainties, the grace to ask what You would have us to do, that the Spirit of Wisdom may save us from all false choices, and that in Your light we may see light, and in Your straight path we may not stumble; through Jesus Christ our Lord. *Amen.*

For Trustfulness

O MOST loving Father, who wills us to give thanks for all things, to dread nothing but the loss of You, and to cast all our care on You and who cares for us; Preserve us from faithless fears and worldly anxieties, and grant that no clouds of this mortal life may hide from us the light of that love which is immortal, and which You have manifested to us in Your Son, Jesus Christ our Lord. *Amen.*

O HEAVENLY Father, You understand all of Your children; through Your gift of faith we bring our confusion to the light of Your wisdom, and receive the blessed encouragement of Your sympathy, and a clearer knowledge of Your will. Glory be to You for all Your gracious gifts. *Amen.*

For Joy in God's Creation

O HEAVENLY Father, who has filled the world with beauty; Open our eyes to behold your gracious hand in all Your works; that rejoicing in Your whole creation, we may learn to serve You with gladness; for the sake of Him by whom all things were made, Your Son, Jesus Christ our Lord. *Amen.*

For the Children

ALMIGHTY God, heavenly Father, who has blessed us with the joy and care of children; Give us light and strength so to train them, that they may love the things that are true and pure and lovely and of good report, following the example of their Savior Jesus Christ. *Amen.*

For the Absent

O GOD, whose fatherly care reaches to the ends of the earth; We humbly ask You graciously to behold and bless those whom we love, now absent from us. Defend them from all dangers of soul and body; and grant that both they and we, drawing nearer to You, may be bound together by Your love in the communion of your Holy Spirit, and in the fellowship of your saints; through Jesus Christ our Lord. *Amen.*

For Those We Love

ALMIGHTY God, we entrust all who are dear to us to your never-failing care and love, for this life and the life to come; knowing that you are doing for them better things than we can desire or pray for; through Jesus Christ our Lord. Amen.

For the Recovery of a Sick Person

O MERCIFUL God, giver of life and health; Bless, we pray You that Your servant, [*N.*], and those who administer to *him* of your healing gifts; that *he* may be restored to health of body and of mind; through Jesus Christ our Lord. *Amen.*

For One about to undergo an Operation

ALMIGHTY God our heavenly Father, we ask You graciously to comfort Your servant in *his* suffering, and to bless the means made use of for *his* cure. Fill *his* he with confidence, that though *he* be sometime afraid, *he* yet may put his trust in You; through Jesus Christ our Lord. *Amen.*

For a Birthday

WATCH over Your child, O Lord, as *his* days increase; bless and guide *him* wherever *he* may be, keeping *him* unspotted from the world. Strengthen *him* when *he* stands; comfort *him* when discouraged or sorrowful;

raise *him* up if *he* falls; and in *his* heart may your peace which passes understanding abide all the days of *his* life; through Jesus Christ our Lord. *Amen.*

For an Anniversary of One Departed

ALMIGHTY God, we remember this day your faithful servant [N.], and we pray that, having opened to *him* the gates of the life hereafter, you will receive *him* more and more into your joyful service; that *he* may rest until the resurrection, with You and Your servants everywhere, in Your eternal victory; through Jesus Christ our Lord. *Amen.*

For Those in Mental Darkness

O HEAVENLY Father, we ask you to have mercy upon all your children who are living in mental darkness. Restore them to strength of mind and cheerfulness of spirit, and give them health and peace; through Jesus Christ our Lord. *Amen.*

For a Blessing on the Families of the Land

ALMIGHTY God, our heavenly Father, who places us in families; We place in your continual care the homes in which your people dwell. Put far from them every root of bitterness, the desire of vainglory, and the pride of life. Fill them with faith, virtue, knowledge, temperance, patience, godliness. Knit together in constant affection those who, in holy wedlock, have been made one flesh; turn the heart of the fathers to the children, and the heart of the children to the fathers; and so enkindle fervent love among us all, that we be endued with brotherly love; through Jesus Christ our Lord. *Amen.*

For all Poor, Homeless, and the Neglected

O GOD, Almighty and merciful, who heals those that are broken in heart, and turns the sadness of the sorrowful to joy; Let Your fatherly goodness be upon all that You have made. Remember in pity those that are destitute, homeless, or forgotten of their fellow-neighbor. Bless the congregation of your poor. Uplift those who are cast down. Mightily befriend innocent sufferers, and sanctify to them the endurance of their wrongs. Cheer with hope all discouraged and unhappy people, and by your heavenly grace preserve from falling those whose extreme poverty tempts them to sin; Although they be troubled on every side, let them not be distressed and though they be perplexed, save them from despair. Grant this, O Lord, for the love of Him, who for our sakes became poor, Your Son, our Savior Jesus Christ. *Amen.*

For Faithfulness in the Use of this World's Goods

ALMIGHTY God, whose loving hand has given us all that we possess; Grant us grace that we may honor you with our substance, and remembering the account which we must one day give, may be faithful stewards of Your bounty; through Jesus Christ our Lord. *Amen.*

A General Intercession

O GOD, at whose word we go to our work and to our vocation until the evening; Be merciful to all whose duties are difficult or burdensome, and comfort them concerning their toil. Shield from bodily accident and harm the employees at their work. Protect the efforts of sober and honest industry, and allow not laborers to be defrauded. Incline the heart of employers and of those whom they employ to mutual patience, fairness, and goodwill. Give the spirit of governance and of a sound mind to all in places of authority. Bless all those who labor in works of mercy. Care for all elderly persons, all little children, the sick and the afflicted, and those who travel. Remember all who by reason of weakness are overtasked, or because of poverty are forgotten. Let the sorrowful sighing of the prisoners come before You; and according to the greatness of Your power, preserve those that are appointed to die. Give ear unto our prayer, O merciful and gracious Father, for the love of Your dear Son, our Savior Jesus Christ. *Amen.*

Grace before Meat

BLESS, O Father, Your gifts to our use and us to your service; for Christ's sake. *Amen.*

GIVE us grateful hearts, our Father, for all Your mercies, and make us mindful of the needs of others; through Jesus Christ our Lord. *Amen.*

PART THREE

EDITOR'S NOTE:

The following prayers were never officially included within the *Book of Common Prayer* but were commonly bound with it. The following prayers derive from three sources, namely a 1567 edition of the *Book of Common Prayer*, as reprinted in the 1847 work, *Liturgical Services in the Reign of Queen Elizabeth* and two versions of the *Book of Common Prayer* published in 1599 and 1634, respectfully. Additionally, these prayers were bound with the 1559 *Book of Common Prayer* in substantially the same form as found in the 1567 edition.

They have been edited by my hand to make them more likely to be used once again in the homes of faithful Anglicans. These prayers are much longer than how we moderns typically pray, but they are also much richer in content. Take your time in praying them and read them first before praying them slowly. May they enrich your faith as much as they have deepened my own.

- *Dcn. A.E. Brashier*

GODLY PRAYERS
CERTAIN GODLY PRAYERS TO BE USED FOR VARIOUS PURPOSES

A general confession of sins, to be said every morning

O ALMIGHTY God, our heavenly Father, I confess, that I am a miserable and a wretched sinner, and have severely transgressed your godly commandments, through wicked thoughts, ungodly lusts, sinful words and deeds, and in my whole life. In sin I am born and conceived, and there is no goodness in me. If you were to enter into judgment upon me, I would never be able to survive it, but would be condemned and damned forever. So little help, comfort, or relief is there within me, or in anyone else. Only this is my comfort O heavenly Father, that you did not spare your only dearly beloved Son, but did give him up unto the most bitter, and most vile and slanderous death of the Cross for me, that He might so pay the ransom for my sins, satisfy your judgment, still and pacify your wrath, reconcile me to You, and purchase your grace and your favor, and everlasting life. Wherefore, through the merit of his most bitter death and passion, and through his innocent blood shedding, I ask you, O heavenly Father, that You will be gracious and merciful to me, forgive and pardon all my sins, to lighten my heart with your Holy Spirit, to renew, confirm, and strengthen me with a right and a perfect faith, and to inflame within me love toward you and my neighbor, that I may now willingly and gladly live in your most godly commandments, and so glorify and praise you everlastingly. And, that I may with a free conscience and quiet heart, in all manner of temptations, afflictions, or necessities, and even in the very pangs of death, cry boldly and joyfully to you, and say:

I believe in God the Father Almighty, maker of heaven and earth,

And in Jesus Christ, his only Son our Lord. Who was conceived by the Holy Ghost, Born of the Virgin Mary, Suffered under Pontius Pilate, Was crucified, dead, and buried; He descended into hell; The third day he rose again from the dead; He ascended into heaven, And sitteth on the right hand of God the Father Almighty; From thence he shall come to judge the quick and the dead.

I believe in the Holy Ghost; The holy Catholic Church; The Communion of Saints; The Forgiveness of sins; The Resurrection of the body, And the Life everlasting. Amen.

But, O Lord God, heavenly Father, to comfort myself in affliction and temptation with the Apostles' Creed, it is not in my power, for faith is Your gift: and I pray and call upon you, O Lord, to please provide for my necessities, as your beloved Son, our Savior, Jesus Christ has taught us. And from the very depth of my soul I cry, and say:

OUR Father who art in heaven, Hallowed be thy name. Thy kingdom come. Thy will be done on earth as it is in heaven. Give us this day our daily bread, and forgive us our trespasses, as we forgive those who trespass against us, and lead us not into temptation, but deliver us from evil. For thine is the kingdom, and the power, and the glory, for ever and ever. *Amen.*

Prayers to be said in the Morning

O MERCIFUL Lord God, heavenly Father, I give you most high praise and thank you, that you have preserved me both this night, and all the time and days of my life, under your protection, and have allowed me to live until this present hour. And I wholeheartedly ask that You will receive me this day, and the rest of my life, from here forevermore into your protection, ruling and governing me with your Holy Spirit, that all manner of darkness, of misbelief, infidelity, and of carnal lusts and affections, may be completely chased and driven out of my heart, and that I may be justified and saved both in body and soul through a right and a perfect faith, and so walk in the light of your most godly truth, to your glory and praise, and to the benefit of my neighbor, through Jesus Christ our Lord and Savior. *Amen.*

ALL possible thanks that we are able, we give to you, O Lord Jesus Christ, for that you have protected us this past night; and we ask you likewise to assist us in using the day for your glory, and for the health of our soul: and that you which are the true light and which are the Son eternal, giving life, food, and gladness for all things, grant to shine into our minds, that we may not anywhere stumble to fall into any sin, but may through your good guidance and directing, come to the life everlasting. *Amen.*

O LORD Jesus Christ, the true Sun of the world, forever rising and never going down, which by your most wholesome appearing and sight, do bring forth, preserve, nourish, and refresh all things, in heaven and on earth; we mercifully ask you to shine into our hearts darkened by sin, and drive away all our errors as you brightly shine within our hearts, so that we may all our life go without any stumbling or offence, and may decently walk in purity from the works of darkness, and abound in the good works which God has prepared for us to walk in; who with the Father and with the Holy Spirit lives and reigns for ever and ever. *Amen*.

O GOD and Lord Jesus Christ, you know and taught us how great the frailties and weaknesses of man is, and how certain it is we can do nothing without your help. Mankind trusts himself by nature and therefore runs and falls headlong into a thousand undoings and mischiefs. Our Father, have pity and compassion upon the weakness of us your children, be willing and ready to help us, always showing mercy upon us, and give us light that we may see what is truly good; Encourage us that we may have an earnest desire to do good; and walk in your ways: for we have nothing but mistrust in ourselves and do surrender ourselves fully and wholly unto you alone, who works all things in creation, to your honor and glory. *Amen*.

A prayer against temptation

O LORD Jesus Christ, the one who maintains our life, our only hope, our only salvation, our glory, and our triumph, who for our sake became human and allowed yourself to be tempted by Satan, and who alone of all mankind did utterly overcome and vanquish sin, death, the world, the Devil, and all the kingdom of hell; and whatever you have commanded, for our well-being you commanded it; you have fought the battle and won it for us and graciously reward us with a crown of the glory for your victory. And in order to overthrow Satan within ourselves, as you have done in your own Person, give us your strength against the roaring Lion, which continually wanders and seeks whom he may devour. You are the Serpent on the staff of Moses that truly gives health and life, that was nailed on high upon a tree, and provides us willingness against the deceits of the most subtle serpent who lurks in the garden of Eden. You are the Lamb who is white as snow, the vanquisher of Satan's tyranny, give us, your little sheep, the strength and virtue of your spirit, that being in our own selves weak and feeble, and in you strong and valiant, we may withstand and overcome all assaults of the Devil, so that our enemy may not glory on us, but being conquered through you, we may give thanks to your mercy, which never leaves them destitute that put their trust in you: who lives and reigns God for ever without end. *Amen.*

A prayer for the obtaining of wisdom

O GOD of Abraham, Isaac, and Jacob, and Lord of mercy, you made all things with your Word, and ordained mankind through your wisdom, that man should have dominion over the creatures which you have made, that man should order the world according to equity and righteousness, and execute judgment with a true heart; give me wisdom and do not exile me: for I your servant am a feeble person, of a short life, and too young understand your judgments and laws: although no person is perfect among the children of men, yet if your wisdom is not with us, we have nothing. O send your wisdom out of heaven, and from the throne of your majesty, that wisdom may be with me and labor with me, that I may know what is acceptable in your sight; for wisdom knows and understands all things, and wisdom shall guide me into your works, and preserve me in your power: so make my works be acceptable to You. *Amen.*

A prayer against worldly cares

O MOST dear and tender Father, our defender and nourisher, fill us with your grace, that we may cast off the great blindness of our minds, and caring about worldly things, and may put our whole study and care in keeping of your holy law; and that we may labor for our necessities in this life, like the birds of the air, and the lilies of the field, without care. For you have promised to care for us, and have commanded that upon you we should cast all our care. Praise be our God who lives and reigns, world without end. *Amen.*

A prayer necessary for all persons

O MERCIFUL God, although I am a wretched sinner I am bound to keep your holy commandments but unable to keep them, and require the righteousness of Jesus Christ your only Son, who has perfectly fulfilled your law, to justify all men who believe and trust in him. Therefore, grant me grace to perform good works, which you command in Holy Scripture, all the days of my life, to your glory, and to trust only in your mercy, and by Christ's merits, to be purged from my sins, and not in my good works. Give me grace to love your Holy Word fervently, to search the Scriptures diligently, to read them humbly, to understand them truly, to live after them effectually. Order my life, O Lord, that it be always acceptable to you. Give me grace not to rejoice in anything that displease you, but evermore to delight in those things that please you. Teach me to pray so that my petitions may be graciously heard by you. Keep me upright among diverse opinions and judgments that I never swerve from your truth taught in Holy Scripture. In prosperity, O Lord, save me, that I become not proud. In adversity help me, that I never despair nor blaspheme your holy Name, but patiently endure, give you thanks, and trust to be delivered as you will. When I happen to fall into sin through frailty, I ask you to work true repentance in my heart, that I may be sorry without desperation, trust in your mercy without presumption, that I may amend my life, and become truly religious without hypocrisy, lowly in heart without reluctantly willing, faithful and trusting without deceit, merry without lightness, sad without mistrust, sober without slothfulness, content with mine own without covetousness, to tell my neighbor his faults charitably without concealment, to instruct my household in your laws, to obey our government without reluctance, to receive all laws (which do not disagree with your Holy Word) obediently, to pay every man that which I owe, to neither gossip nor slander my neighbor secretly, and to abhor all vice, loving all goodness earnestly. O Lord, grant me the will to do these things, for the glory of your holy Name. *Amen.*

A prayer necessary to be said at all times

O BOUNTIFUL Jesus, O sweet savior, O Christ the Son of God, have pity upon me, mercifully hear me, and despise not my prayers. You have created me from nothing, you have redeemed me from the bondage of sin, death, and hell, neither with gold nor silver, but with your most precious body once offered upon the cross, and your own blood shed once for all for my ransom; therefore cast me not away, whom your by your great wisdom has made: despise me not, whom you have redeemed with such a precious treasure. Nor let my wickedness destroy that, which your goodness has built. Now while I live, O Jesus have mercy on me, for if I die outside of your favor, it will be too late afterward to call for your mercy. While I have time to repent, look upon me with your merciful eyes, as you did look upon Peter your Apostle, that I may lament my sinful life, and obtain your favor, and die therein. I acknowledge, that if you should deal with me according to very justice, I deserve everlasting death. Therefore, I appeal to your high throne of mercy trusting to obtain God's favor, not by my merits, but through your merits, Jesus, who has given yourself as an acceptable sacrifice to your Father, to appease his wrath, and to bring all sinners, (truly repenting and amending their evil life) into his favor again. Accept me, O Lord, among the number of them that shall be saved, forgive my sins, give me grace to lead a godly and innocent life, grant me your heavenly wisdom, inspire my heart with faith, hope, and charity; give me grace to be humble in prosperity, patient in adversity, obedient to my rulers, faithful unto them that trust me, dealing truly with all men, to live faithfully in marriage, to abhor adultery, fornication, and all uncleanness, to do good to all men, to hurt no man, that your name may be glorified in me, during this present life, and that I afterward may obtain everlasting life, through your mercy, and the merits of your passion. *Amen.*

Miscellaneous Daily Prayers

Monday

ALMIGHTY God, the Father of mercy, and God of all comfort, who alone forgives sin, forgive us our sins, good Lord, forgive us our sins; that by the multitude of your mercies they may be covered, and not imputed to us, and by the operation of the Holy Spirit, we may have power and strength hereafter to resist sin through our Savior and Lord Jesus Christ. *Amen.*

Tuesday.

O LORD GOD, who despises not a contrite heart, and forgets the sins and wickedness of a sinner when he does grieve and lament his old manner of living; grant to us O Lord true contrition of heart, that we may vehemently despise our sinful past life, and wholly be converted to you, by our Savior and Lord Jesus Christ. *Amen.*

Wednesday.

O MERCIFUL FATHER, by whose power and strength we may overcome our enemies both in body and spirit: grant to us, O Lord, that, according to the promise made in our baptism, we may overcome the chief enemies of our soul, that is, the desires of the world, the pleasures of the flesh, and the suggestions of the Devil; and so after lead our lives in holiness and righteousness, that we may serve you in spirit and truth, by our Savior and Lord Jesus Christ. *Amen.*

Thursday.

O ALMIGHTY and everlasting God, who not only gives every good and perfect gift, but also increases those gifts that you have given; we most humbly ask you merciful God to increase in us the gift of faith, that we may truly believe in you, and in your promises made to us; and that neither by our negligence, nor infirmity of the flesh, nor by temptation, neither by the subtle crafts and assaults of the Devil we be driven from faith in the blood of our Savior and Lord Jesus Christ. *Amen*.

Friday.

GRANT to us, O merciful God, knowledge and true understanding of your Word, and expel our ignorance so we may know what your will and pleasure is in all things, and how to do our duties, and truly to walk in our vocation, and that we may live faithfully, that we not merely know your Word, good Lord, but also be doers of the Word; through our Savior and Lord Jesus Christ. *Amen*.

Saturday

O ALMIGHTY God, who prepared everlasting life to all those that are faithful servants: grant to us, Lord, sure hope of the life everlasting, that we, being in this miserable world, may have some taste and feeling it in our hearts; by the merits of our Savior and Lord Jesus Christ. *Amen*.

O MERCIFUL God, our only aide, relief, and strength at all times; grant unto us, O Lord, that in the time of prosperity we be not proud and forget you, but that with our whole power and strength we cleave unto you; and in the time of adversity, that we fall not to infidelity and desperation, but always with a constant faith we call for our help, grant this, O Lord, for the sake of our Savior Jesus Christ. *Amen.*

Sunday.

O ALMIGHTY and merciful Lord, who gives to your elect people the Holy Spirit, as a sure pledge of your heavenly kingdom; Grant unto us, O Lord, your Holy Spirit, that he may bear witness with our spirit, that we be your children, and heirs of your kingdom, and that by the operation of your Spirit we may kill all carnal lusts, unlawful pleasures, debased longings, and evil affections contrary to your will, by our Savior and Lord Jesus Christ. *Amen.*

A prayer for trust in God

The beginning of the fall of man was trust in himself. The beginning of the restoring of man, was distrust in himself, and trust in God. O most gracious and most wise guide, our Savior Christ, who does lead us in the right way to immortal blessedness, who truly and sincerely trust in you, commit themselves to you; Grant us, that since we are blind and feeble in deed, help us to refuse ourselves, so we trust not in ourselves, but that we always may have you before our eyes, to follow you, being our guide, to be ready and obedient at your call, and to commit ourselves wholly to you; that you, who is the Way, may lead us to heavenly desires; to You with the Father and the Holy Spirit be glory forever. Amen.

A prayer for the concord of Christ's church

ARISE Lord, let your enemies be scattered, your haters put to flight, so the righteous and Christ's disciples might be pleasant and merry, let them sing praises and pleasant songs to you, let them proclaim abroad your magnificence, let them most highly advance your majesty, let your glory grow, let the kingdom of Christ from heaven among the chosen be enlarged. Be the Father of the fatherless, the judge of the widowers, and the protector of them, especially those whom the world forsake, whose consciences are troubled, whom the world pursued for Christ's sake, which are wrapped full of misery. In your house O Lord, let us dwell in peace and concord, give us all one heart, one mind, one true interpretation of your Word. Remove the bonds from our consciences as from the bodies of the miserable captives and of them also which are nearing death who sadly strive against grace. I pray, pour down largely the showers of your graces and make us fruitful with good works, let your people be strengthened with your Spirit. Grant us Lord your Word abundantly, so that there may be many preachers of your Gospel. Let the church, the spouse of Christ, deliver blows to the conquered Satan. All that believe in you by Christ, O Lord God of health, may they lift You up with praises, might know you and extol you. We are on the voyage of salvation. Conduct us safely into the port, that being delivered by You from the verge of death, we may escape and come to true life. Finish the thing that you have begun in us, make us to increase from faith to faith, leave us not to our own will and decisions, for we are slippery and ready to fall. We give the glory to You alone. Give to your people courage and power to withstand sin, and to obey your word in all things O Lord God, most glorious and excellent King over all. *Amen.*

A prayer against the enemies of Christ's truth

DELIVER me O Lord, from the ungodly and stiff-necked persons, for you see how in their hearts they imagine mischief, and have great pleasure to pick quarrels, their tongues are sharper than any snakebite, and under their lips hold poison of snakes. But, O merciful Lord, let me not fall into their hands, that they handle not me after their own lusts. You alone are my God, you must hear my pious complaint Lord for you are the strength and power of my defense. Be for me a helmet on my head when the ungodly shall assault me. Do not allow the wicked to prosper in their evil. Do not allow their crooked and malicious ways increase. Look upon your children with mercy, and rid me of these daily grievances, then shall I with an upright heart and pleasant face praise and magnify your holy Name. *Amen.*

A prayer for patience in trouble

You O Lord humbled and plucked me down. I scarcely make my prayers to you, for you are angry with me and not without my deserving. Certainly I have sinned, Lord, I confess it; I will not deny it; but, oh my God, pardon my trespasses, release my debts, render now your grace again unto me, stop my wounds, for I am plagued and beaten; yet Lord this notwithstanding I abide patiently, and give mine attention to you, continually waiting for relief at your hand; for I have received a token of your favor and grace towards me, namely your word of promise concerning Christ, who for me was offered on the Cross for a ransom, a sacrifice and price for my sins; wherefore, according to your promise, defend me Lord by your right hand, and give a gracious ear to my requests, for all of our ways are but vain. Beat down therefore the evil one with your power, as you are my only aide and protector, O Lord God almighty. *Amen.*

A prayer to be said at night going to bed

O MERCIFUL Lord God, heavenly Father, whether we sleep or wake, live or die, we are always yours. I ask you heartily that you will promise to take care and oversee me, and not allow me to perish in the works of darkness, but to kindle the light of your face in my heart, that your godly knowledge may increase daily in me, through a right and pure faith, and that I may always live after your will and pleasure, through Jesus Christ our Lord and Savior. *Amen.*

A prayer to be said at the hour of death

O LORD Jesus, who is the only health of all living, and the everlasting life of them which die in faith. I, a wretched sinner, give and commit myself wholly to your most blessed will. And I being sure that I will not perish due to your great mercy, leave this frail and sinful flesh, in hope of the resurrection, which shall soon restore me to life. I beg you, most merciful Lord Jesus Christ, that your will and by your grace make my soul strong against all temptations, and that you will cover and defend me with your mercy against all the assaults of the Devil. I see and acknowledge, that there is within me no help of salvation, but all my confidence, hope, and trust, is in your most merciful goodness. I have no merits, nor good works, which I may lay before you. I carry a load of sins and evil works, but through your mercy, I trust to be in the number of those whom your will not impute their sins, but take and accept me as righteous and just, and to be the inheritor of everlasting life. You, merciful Lord, was born for my sake, you did suffer both hunger and thirst for my sake, you did preach and teach, you did pray and fast for my sake, you did all good works and deeds for my sake, you suffered most grievous pains and torments for my sake. And finally, you gave your most precious body to die, and your blood to be shed on the cross for my sake. Now, most merciful Savior, let all these things benefit me, which you freely have given me. Let your blood cleanse and wash away the spots and foulness of my sins. Let your righteousness hide and cover my unrighteousness. Let the merits of your passion and blood, be the satisfaction for my sins. Give me Lord you grace, that my faith and salvation in your blood wavers not in me, but be ever firm and constant, that the hope of your mercy and life everlasting never decay in me, and that charity become not cold in me. Finally, may the weakness of my flesh be not overcome with the fear of death. Grant me, merciful Savior, that when death has shut up the eyes of my body, yet the eyes of my soul may still behold and look upon You; that when death has taken away the use of my tongue and speech, yet my heart may cry and say unto You, O Lord, into your hands I give and commit my soul; Lord Jesus, receive my soul unto You, Amen. *Amen.*

Another prayer for the Morning

O Most Almighty and most gracious God, we thank you for the sweet sleep and comfortable rest which you have given us this night; and as You have commanded by Your holy Word that no man should be idle, but all occupied in godly and virtuous exercises, every man according to his calling; we most humbly ask You, that Your eyes look upon us, daily defend us, cherish, comfort, and govern us and all our deliberations, studies, and labors that we may spend this day according to Your most holy will, without hurting our neighbors, and that we may diligently and warily have nothing to do with and avoid all things that should displease You set Yourself always before our eyes, to live in your fear, while working that which may be found acceptable before your divine Majesty, through Christ our Lord. *Amen.*

A prayer for the Evening

O Most mighty Lord our Father, and God everlasting, full of pity and compassion, we acknowledge and confess, that we are not worthy to lift up our eyes to heaven, much less to present ourselves before your Majesty, with confidence that You will hear our prayers, and grant our requests, if we consider our own deserving; For our consciences does accuse us, and our sins witness against us, and we know that you are an upright Judge, who does not justify the sinners and wicked men, but punishes the faults of such as transgress your Commandments. Yet most merciful Father, since it has pleased You to command us to call upon You in all out troubles and adversities, promising even then to help us, when we feel ourselves swallowed up by death and desperation; we utterly renounce all worldly confidence, and flee to your Sovereign abundance, as our only stay and refuge, asking You not to call to remembrance our manifold sins and wickedness, where we continually provoke your wrath and indignation against us, neither our negligence and unkindness, which have neither worthily esteemed, nor in our lives sufficiently expressed the sweet comfort of your Gospel revealed unto us, but rather accept the obedience and death of your Son Jesus Christ, who by offering by his body in sacrifice once for all, has made sufficient payment for all our sins. Have mercy therefore upon us, O Lord, and forgive us our offences. Teach us by your Holy Spirit, that we may rightly weigh them, and earnestly repent for the same; and O Lord, because the reprobate cannot praise You, nor call upon your Name; but the repenting heart, the sorrowful mind, the conscience oppressed, hungering and thirsting for your grace, shall ever proclaim your praise and glory. And although we are worms and dust, yet You are our Creator, and we are the work of your hands. Yes, You are our Father, and we are your children; You are our Shepherd, and we are your flock: You are our Redeemer, and we are the people whom You have bought: You are our God and we are your inheritance. Correct us not in your anger, O Lord, neither punish according to what we deserve, but mercifully discipline us with a fatherly affection, that all the world may know that when a sinner does repent of his sin from the bottom of his heart, You will put away his wickedness out of your memory, as You have promised by your holy Prophet.

Finally, inasmuch as it has pleased You to make the night for man to rest in, as You have ordained him the day to toil in; Grant, O dear Father, that we may so take our bodily rest, that our souls may continually watch for the time that our Lord Jesus Christ shall appear for our deliverance out of this mortal life, and that we may fully set our minds upon You, love You, revere You, and rest in You. Furthermore, that our minds are not distracted or focused on the ravenous desires of our flesh, but direct our minds and hearts, in spite of our weak nature, to be better focused to live in godly behavior, to the glory of your holy Name, and benefit of our neighbors. *Amen.*

The prayer of Manasseh King of the Jews

O Lord Almighty, God of our fathers, Abraham, Isaac, and Jacob, and of their righteous seed, who has made heaven and earth with all its detailed beauty, who has bound the Sea by the word of your command, who has shut up the deep and sealed it by your terrible and glorious Name, whom in all do fear, and tremble before your power; for the Majesty of your glory is unbearable, and your anger toward sinners is unendurable, but your merciful promise is unmeasurable and unsearchable. For You are the most high Lord, of great compassion, long suffering, and most merciful and repents for man's miseries. You, O Lord, according to Your great goodness you promised repentance and forgiveness to those that sin against You, and for your infinite mercies You have appointed repentance unto sinners, that we may be saved. You therefore, O Lord, who is the God of the just, have not appointed repentance to the just, such as Abraham, Isaac, and Jacob, who have not sinned against You, but You have appointed repentance unto me as I am a sinner. For I have sinned above the number of the sand of the Sea. My transgressions, O Lord, are multiplied, my transgressions are exceeding many, and I am not worthy to behold and see your heavenly presence due to the multitude of my unrighteousness. My back is bent with the weight of my sins, that I cannot lift up my head, and I have no relief; For I have provoked your wrath and done evil before You. I did not do your will, neither have I kept your Commandments. I have set up abominations and have multiplied offences. Now therefore I bow the knee of my heart, asking for Your grace. I have sinned, O Lord, I have sinned, and I acknowledge my transgressions; but I humbly ask You, forgive me; O Lord forgive me, and destroy me not with my transgressions. Be not angry with me forever, by reserving evil for me, neither condemn me unto the lower parts of the earth. For You are God, even the God of those who repent; and in me You will show all your goodness; for You will save the unworthy, according to your great mercy. Therefore, I will praise You forever all the days of my life. For all the powers of the heavens praise You, and yours is the glory for ever and ever. *Amen.*

A Prayer containing the duty of every true Christian

O Most mighty GOD, merciful and loving Father, I am a wretched sinner coming to You in the Name of your dearly beloved Son Jesus Christ, my only Savior and Redeemer. I most humbly ask You for Christ's sake to be merciful to me, and to cast all my sins out of your sight and memory through the merits of His bloody death and Passion. Pour upon me, O Lord, the holy Spirit of wisdom and grace; govern and lead me by your holy Word, that it may be a lantern unto my feet, and a light unto my steps. Show your mercy upon me, and so lighten my natural blindness and darkness of my heart through your grace, that I may daily be renewed by Your Holy Spirit. O Lord purge the deafness of my hearing and understanding, that I may profitably read, hear, and understand the word and your heavenly will, and then to believe and practice the same in my life and behavior, and evermore hold fast that blessed hope of everlasting life.

Mortify and kill all vice in me, that my life may express my faith in You; mercifully hear the humble prayers of your servant and grant me your peace all my days. Graciously pardon my infirmities, and defend me in all dangers of body, goods, and name; but most chiefly protect my soul against all assaults, temptations, accusations, subtle baits, and deceptions from the old enemy of mankind, Satan that roaring Lion, who is always seeking whom he may devour.

And here, O Lord, I prostrate with most humble mind and crave your divine Majesty to be merciful to the universal Church of your Son Jesus Christ; and ask

You for His sake to bless, save, guide, and defend the [*President/Prime Minister*], increase in *him/her* the true faith, godly zeal, and love of the same; And grant *him/her* victory over all enemies, a long, prosperous, and honorable life upon earth, a blessed end, and life everlasting.

Moreover, O Lord, grant to the [*President/Prime Minister*]'s cabinet, and every other member of this Church, that together we may truly and godly serve You. Plant in our hearts true fear and honor of your Name, obedience to our political leaders, and love to our neighbors; Increase in us true Faith and Religion; Replenish our minds with goodness, and of your great mercy keep us in the Faith until the end of our lives. Give unto us a godly zeal in prayer, true humility in prosperity, perfect patience in adversity, and continual joy in the Holy Spirit.

And lastly, I commend unto your Fatherly protection, all that You have given me, namely *my wife and children.* Aid me, O Lord, that I may govern, nourish, and bring them up in your fear and service. And as in this world I must always be at war and strife, not only with one flesh and blood, but with the devil, the prince of darkness, and with the wicked men who perform his most damnable will. Grant me therefore your grace, that being armed with your defense, I may stand in the battle and persevere against all corruption which I am surrounded by on every side, until in the end I may attain to your heavenly rest, which is prepared for me and all your Elect, through Christ our Lord and only Savior. *Amen.*

Part Four

THE CLASSIC BOOK OF COMMON PRAYER CATECHISM – A MODERNIZED TEXT

This catechism has been slightly modernized in its text to assist young Christians learning the requirements for admission to communion. The 2019 ACNA *Book of Common Prayer* does not contain the classic rubric from the 1662 *Book of Common Prayer* and 1928 U.S. *Book of Common Prayer*, that:

> *And there shall none be admitted to the holy Communion, until such time as he be confirmed, or be ready and desirous to be confirmed.*

Although this rubric is not included in the 2019 ACNA prayer book, it is arguably still in force as the ACNA Constitution upholds the 1662 *Book of Common Prayer* "as a standard for Anglican doctrine and discipline."[9] Therefore, this disciplinary rubric from the 1662 prayer book is arguably enforceable in the ACNA, or in the very least, provides proper doctrinal guidance as to who shall be administered Holy Communion.[10] Regardless, the classic prayer books and the ACNA prayer book require all confirmands to learn "the

---

[9] *See* ACNA Constitution, Art.I.6; *see also*, ACNA 2019 *Book of Common Prayer*, Fundamental Declarations, p. 767 (quoting the same).

[10] For a more detailed explanation of this line of reasoning, *see* Brashier, Andrew. "Common Authority in the Midst of Uncommon Prayer." *The North American Anglican*, (Aug. 11, 2019) (available at: http://northamanglican.com/common-authority-in-the-midst-of-uncommon-prayer/).

Creed, the Lord's Prayer, the Ten Commandments." The classic prayer books point to the "short Catechism" within the prayer book as the source to learn these three requirements while the ACNA requires instruction from its longer Catechism, to be finalized and published in 2020.

Unfortunately, the classic prayer book short Catechism was not republished in the 1979 *Book of Common Prayer* but was instead wholly rewritten. Meanwhile, the ACNA *Book of Common Prayer* does not include any catechism as it is publishing a separate catechism that is more comprehensive and geared towards explaining the Christian faith in detail to those without a background in the church and are new to the faith. Therefore, in an effort to assist parents of young children who wish to have a more concise and classic catechism to teach their children the fundamentals required for confirmation and communion I have slightly edited the catechism from the 1662 and 1928 editions of the *Book of Common Prayer*.

A Catechism
that is to say, an Instruction,
to be Learned by Every Person before he
be brought to be Confirmed
by the Bishop.

Question. What is your Name?

Answer. *Name or First Name, Last Name.*

Question. Who gave you this Name?

Answer. My Sponsors [or God-parents] in Baptism; when I was made a member of Christ, a child of God, and an inheritor of the kingdom of heaven.

Question. What did your Sponsors do for you?

Answer. They promised and vowed three things in my name: First, that I should renounce the devil and all his works, the arrogance and vanity of this wicked world, and all the sinful lusts of the flesh; Secondly, that I should believe all the Articles of the Christian Faith; And Thirdly, that I should keep God's holy will and commandments, and walk in them all the days of my life.

Question. Do you not think that you are obligated to believe, and to do as they have promised for you?

Answer. Yes, truly; and by God's help I will. And I heartily thank our heavenly Father, that he has called me to salvation, through Jesus Christ our Savior. And I pray to God to give me his grace, that I may continue in salvation to my life's end.

Catechist. Rehearse the Articles of your Belief.

Answer. I believe in God the Father Almighty, Maker of heaven and earth;

And in Jesus Christ, his only Son our Lord; Who was conceived by the Holy Ghost, Born of the Virgin Mary; Suffered under Pontius Pilate, Was crucified, dead, and buried; He descended into hell; The third day he rose again from the dead; He ascended into heaven, And sitteth on the right hand of God the Father Almighty; From thence he shall come to judge the quick and the dead.

I believe in the Holy Ghost; The holy Catholic Church; The Communion of Saints; The Forgiveness of sins; The Resurrection of the body; And the Life everlasting. Amen.

Question. What do you chiefly learn in these Articles of your Belief?

Answer. First, I learn to believe in God the Father, who has made me, and all the world.

Second, in God the Son, who has redeemed me, and all mankind.

Third, in God the Holy Spirit, who sanctifies me, and all the elect people of God.

Question. You said that your Sponsors did promise for you, that you should keep God's Commandments. How many are there?

Answer. Ten.

Question. What are they?

Answer. The same which God spoke in the twentieth Chapter of Exodus, saying, "I am the LORD your God, who brought you out of the land of Egypt, out of the house of slavery."

I. You shall have no other gods before me.

II. You shall not make for yourself a carved image, or any likeness of anything that is in heaven above, or that is in the earth beneath, or that is in the water under the earth. You shall not bow down to them or serve them, for I, the Lord your God, am a jealous God, visiting the iniquity of the fathers on the children to the third and the fourth generation of those who hate me, but showing steadfast love to thousands of those who love me and keep my commandments.

III. You shall not take the name of the Lord your God in vain, for the Lord will not hold him guiltless who takes his name in vain.

IV. Remember the Sabbath day, to keep it holy. Six days you shall labor, and do all your work, but the seventh day is a Sabbath to the Lord your God. On it you shall not do any work, you, or your son, or your daughter, your male servant, or your female servant, or your livestock, or the sojourner who is within your gates. For in six days the Lord made heaven and earth, the sea, and all that is in them, and rested on the seventh day. Therefore the Lord blessed the Sabbath day and made it holy.

V. Honor your father and your mother, that your days may be long in the land that the Lord your God is giving you.

VI. You shall not murder.

VII. You shall not commit adultery.

VIII. You shall not steal.

IX. You shall not bear false witness against your neighbor.

X. You shall not covet your neighbor's house; you shall not covet your neighbor's wife, or his male servant, or his female servant, or his ox, or his donkey, or anything that is your neighbor's.

Question. What do you chiefly learn through these Commandments?

Answer. I learn two things; my duty towards God, and my duty towards my Neighbor.

Question. What is your duty towards God?

Answer. My duty towards God is to believe in him, to fear him, and to love him with all my heart, with all my mind, with all my soul, and with all my strength; To worship him, to give him thanks; To put my whole trust in him, to call upon him; To honor his holy Name and his Word; and to serve him truly all the days of my life.

Question. What is your duty towards your Neighbor?

Answer. My duty towards my Neighbor is to love him as myself, and treat all men as I would hope they treat me; to love, honor, and aid my father and mother; to honor and obey the civil authority; to submit myself to all my governors, teachers, spiritual pastors and masters; to act respectfully to those in my charge; to hurt nobody in my words or deeds; to be truthful and just in all I do; to bear no ill-will or hatred in my heart; to keep my hands from stealing, and my tongue from evil speaking, lying, and slandering; to keep my body in temperance, soberness, and chastity; not to covet nor desire the possessions of others; but to learn and labor to make my living; and to do my duty in the vocations that God calls and places me.

Catechist. My good Child, know this; that you are not able to do these things on your own, nor to walk in the Commandments of God, and serve Him, without His special grace; which you must learn at all times to ask for by diligent prayer. Let me hear, therefore, if you can say the Lord's Prayer.

Answer. Our Father, who art in heaven, Hallowed be thy Name. Thy kingdom come. Thy will be done, On earth as it is in heaven. Give us this day our daily bread. And forgive us our trespasses, As we forgive those who trespass against us. And lead us not into temptation, But deliver us from evil. For thine is the kingdom, and the power, and the glory, for ever and ever. Amen.

Question. What do you desire from God in this Prayer?

Answer. I desire my Lord God, our heavenly Father, who is the giver of all goodness, to send his grace unto me, and to all people; that we may worship him, serve him, and obey him, as we ought to do. And I pray to God, that he will send us all things that are necessary for both our souls and bodies; and that he will be merciful to us, and forgive us our sins; and that it will please him to save and defend us in all dangers both of soul and body; and that he will keep us from all sin and wickedness, and from our spiritual enemy, and from everlasting death. And this I trust he will do of his mercy and goodness, through our Lord Jesus Christ. And therefore, I say, Amen, which means "So be it."

Question. How many Sacraments has Christ ordained in his Church?

Answer. Two only, as generally necessary for salvation; those are Baptism and the Supper of the Lord.

Question. What do you mean by the word Sacrament?

Answer. I mean an outward and visible sign of an inward and spiritual grace given to us; ordained by Christ himself, as a means where we receive the same, and a pledge to assure us.

Question. How many parts are there in a Sacrament?

Answer. Two: the outward visible sign, and the inward spiritual grace.

Question. What is the outward visible sign or form in Baptism?

Answer. Water; where the person is baptized, "In the Name of the Father, and of the Son, and of the Holy Spirit."

Question. What is the inward and spiritual grace?

Answer. A death to our sin, and a new birth into righteousness: for being by nature born in sin, and the children of wrath, we are now made the children of grace.

Question. What is required of persons to be baptized?

Answer. Repentance, where we forsake sin; and Faith, where we loyally believe the promises of God made to us in that Sacrament.

Question. Why are infants baptized, when due to their young age they cannot repent or have faith?

Answer. Because their Sponsors promise on their behalf; which promises, when the infants come to age, themselves are bound to perform.

Question. Why was the Sacrament of the Lord's Supper ordained?

Answer. For the continual remembrance of the sacrifice of the death of Christ, and for the benefits which we receive through it.

Question. What is the outward part or sign of the Lord's Supper?

Answer. Bread and Wine, which the Lord has commanded to be received.

Question. What is the inward part, or thing signified?

Answer. The Body and Blood of Christ, which are truly and certainly taken and received by the faithful in the Lord's Supper.

Question. What are the benefits we partake in through the Lord's Supper?

Answer. The strengthening and refreshing of our souls by the Body and Blood of Christ, just as our bodies are strengthened and refreshed by the Bread and Wine.

Question. What is required of those who come to the Lord's Supper?

Answer. To examine themselves, whether they truly repent of their past sins, firmly intend to lead a new life; have a lively faith in God's mercy through Christ, with a thankful remembrance of his death; and are in charity with all men.

¶ The Minister of every Parish shall diligently, upon Sundays and Holy Days, or on some other convenient occasions, openly in the Church, instruct or examine so many Children of his Parish, sent unto him, as he shall think convenient, in some part of this Catechism.

¶ And all Fathers, Mothers, Stepparents, Guardians, and Godparents, shall cause their Children who have not learned their Catechism, to come to the Church at the time appointed, and obediently hear and be taught by the Minister, until such time as they have learned all that is here appointed for them to learn.

¶ So soon as Children are come to a competent age, and can say the Creed, the Lord's Prayer, and the Ten Commandments, and can answer to the other questions of this short Catechism, they shall be brought to the Bishop.

¶ And whenever the Bishop shall give knowledge for Children to be brought unto him for their Confirmation, the Minister of every Parish shall either bring, or send in writing, with his signature, the Names of all such Persons within his Parish, as he shall think are ready to be confirmed by the Bishop.

Acknowledgements

I want to thank my lovely and beloved wife, Cara, for her unending devotion to our family and her understanding my inability to say "no" to a new project. I find inspiration in my dear daughter, Holland, who has quickly learned the Lord's Prayer and Apostles' Creed thanks to the work of Bishop Edmund Gibson and the foresight of the committee that included many of his family offices in the 1928 *Book of Common Prayer*. I am motivated to write this book for the Church by my son Beckett, whom I hope will learn as quickly as his sister how to recite the key tenets of our faith in preparation for his own confirmation. Already, he is reciting a word here and there with us when we pray the Lord's Prayer.

My appreciation goes to Bishop Gibson, whom I shall see on the other side of eternity and who performed the real work of authoring the majority of these magnificent offices for family and individual use. May the bishops of the Anglican Church learn from his insight that faith begins at home and through regular prayer.

I would be remiss if I did not thank Mr. Charles Bartlett, of the United Episcopal Church. He inspired me to begin my own family oratory and is to be credited for leading me in my research to discovering Bishop Gibson and eventually the "Godly Prayers" originally attached to many editions of the 1559 *Book of Common Prayer*. I commend to the reader his blog,

Anglican Rose, which may be found at www. https://www.anglicanrose.blog/. He is an excellent example at how a family oratory can grow into a church plant. He is a lay reader and the leader of Littlewood UE Chapel, and if you are in the San Francisco area, you should reach out to him. His chapel's website is https://www.fremontanglicans.com.

I thank the Venerable Worth E. Norman, Jr., who graciously edited this work and provided me with the ability to publish this for the glory of God. He is a rock of faith and a pillar of trust whom I rely upon at Anglican Church of the Good Shepherd. He has poked and prodded me along the process of publishing this work. Any errors, I assure the reader, are purely my own.

I give thanks to my bishop, the Right Reverend Derek L.S. Jones for his faith in my ministry and the time he invests in making me a better deacon. I pray your investment in me one day bears much fruit. Thank you, Your Grace.

Last, but not least, I thank my father and mother for raising me in the Church and teaching me through regular attendance in the Methodist church the Lord's Prayer and Apostles' Creed. Your prayers have formed my own prayer life and have been heard by the LORD God as He has rescued me and guided me in my life. Praise the Father, Son, and Holy Ghost, and may this small work benefit His Church and bring glory to the Name of the LORD.

www.ingramcontent.com/pod-product-compliance
Lightning Source LLC
Chambersburg PA
CBHW052101110526
44591CB00013B/2303